9780810 994232
IE737553

lucille reyboz

source

源

PRÉFACE / FOREWORD / 序文

Hitonari Tsuji

ABRAMS, NEW YORK

TO MY `SWEET SAMOURAI´

スウィート サムライに捧ぐ

「女身よりこぼれし月のひと雫」

DE SON CORPS DE FEMME TOMBE UNE GOUTTE DE LUNE
FROM HER BODY DROPS A MOON DRIP

Madoka Mayuzumi

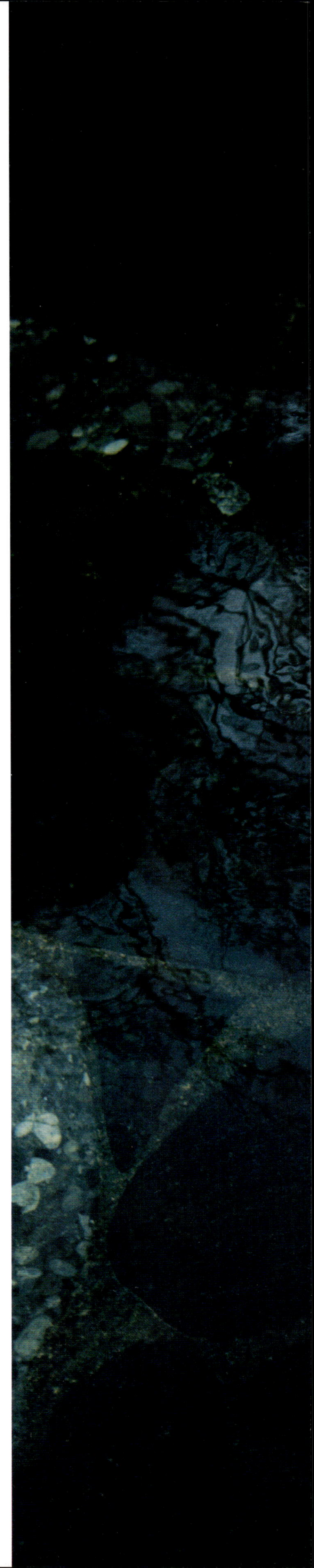

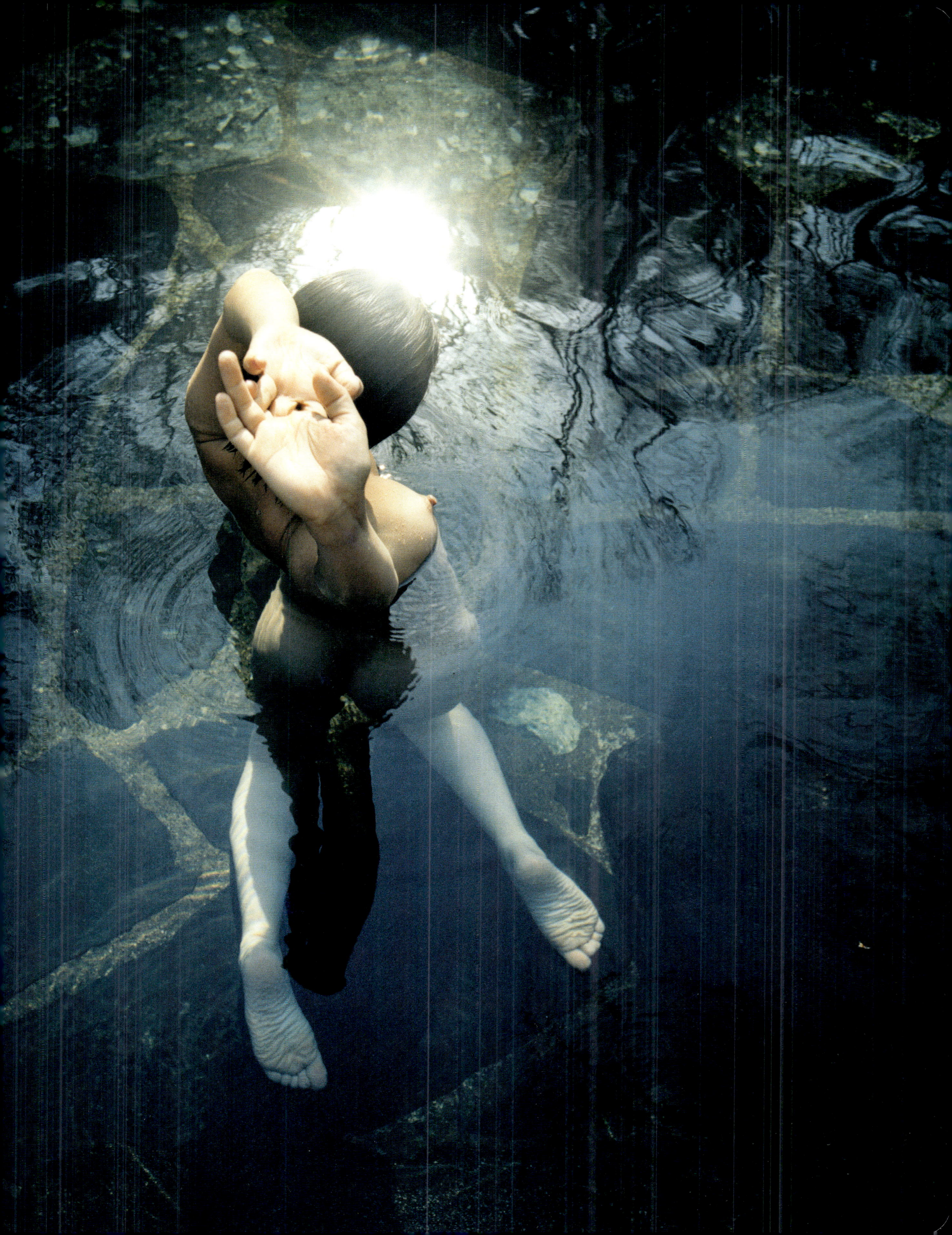

Prière bleue

Le Japon, malgré sa longue tradition et le fait qu'il soit devenu un État moderne, ne possède pas de religion unique comme les pays chrétiens d'Occident ou les pays musulmans du Moyen-Orient. Beaucoup de Japonais fêtent Noël, organisent les funérailles de leurs défunts au temple bouddhiste et se rendent au sanctuaire shintoïste pour prier le premier jour de l'année. Du point de vue religieux, ce peuple n'a aucun principe. Ici et depuis des temps immémoriaux se ressent l'influence d'un animisme qui fait vénérer une nature peuplée de divinités. Les Japonais rendent depuis toujours un culte aux ancêtres et aux dieux de la nature, culte théorisé ultérieurement sous l'influence de pensées extérieures comme le bouddhisme, le confucianisme ou encore le taoïsme. Cette croyance qu'en toute chose réside un esprit ou une existence spirituelle provient sans doute de l'influence exercée par le shintoïsme.

Les photographies prises par Lucille Reyboz m'ont d'emblée donné le sentiment de vouloir capter chez les Japonais ce sentiment animiste face à la nature. Mais si ses images du Japon racontent l'étrange cohabitation d'une vision du monde quasi primitive et d'une technologie de pointe, la photographe a su éviter les clichés trompeurs et toujours de saison autour des *samuraï*, *geisha*, *harakiri* et autre *Sayuri* pour au contraire mettre en relief, avec sensibilité, cette manière de se ressourcer et de se recueillir spirituellement héritée du IIIe siècle, époque où l'impératrice Himiko régnait sur le Yamataikoku.

Cet album a pour décor des sources chaudes (*on-sen*) au Japon et la conception moderne des bains, encore très liée à un animisme de l'eau. Si l'on parle d'*on-sen* pour désigner l'ensemble constitué par les auberges et restaurants édifiés autour des sources, le *on-sen* japonais diffère néanmoins de la station thermale européenne où l'on se rend en cure. Les Japonais fréquentent les *on-sens* pour se baigner. C'est un lieu où l'on vient se ressourcer, corps et esprit. Leur présence sur l'ensemble de l'archipel tient à sa situation au confluent de plusieurs plaques tectoniques, région de séismes où l'activité volcanique reste forte ; à l'évidence, les croyances animistes japonaises, remontant à l'Antiquité, sont directement liées à ce phénomène. Sans doute est-ce ce qui a attiré l'attention de Lucille Reyboz sur les *on-sens*, ces vasques emplies d'eaux chaudes jaillies de la terre évoquant, sous son regard, la matrice originelle.

La construction extrêmement travaillée des images m'a d'abord déconcerté, avant de comprendre que c'était précisément grâce à cette construction que je voyais apparaître la beauté formelle du Japon technologique, que je pouvais ressentir son rythme naturel, autochtone. À la recherche de cet animisme, Lucille a su ne pas s'arrêter aux seules apparences, elle est parvenue à décrire la solitude, l'isolement, les dissensions, les réconciliations, le futur, les symboles, la superficialité, la profondeur du Japon (ais). À travers la sérénité bleue émanant de ses photographies, s'exprime toute la capacité de recueillement de cette artiste.

Dans son livre précédent sur une peuplade africaine vivant à l'écart de la « civilisation », une photographie montrait un enfant tentant de s'extraire d'une pièce par un trou rond, semblable au nouveau-né sortant de l'utérus. Les *on-sens* japonais sont probablement l'image exacte de la cavité utérine située au-delà. On se laisse porter avec bonheur par la puissance critique de cette femme photographe, confrontant avec subtilité les Africains menant cette existence primitive et immuable à cette mentalité animiste des Japonais bioniques immergés jusqu'au cou dans l'eau tiède d'une civilisation technologique.

Devant l'image d'une femme à la chevelure noire et humide, répandue comme une coulée de lave, j'ai compris que Lucille Reyboz avait été profondément troublée par la quête de cette originalité qui fait l'univers psychique des Japonais. C'est une chose que j'éprouve furtivement depuis quelques années, moi le Japonais résidant à Paris, lorsque je me tourne vers mon pays.

Hitonari Tsuji

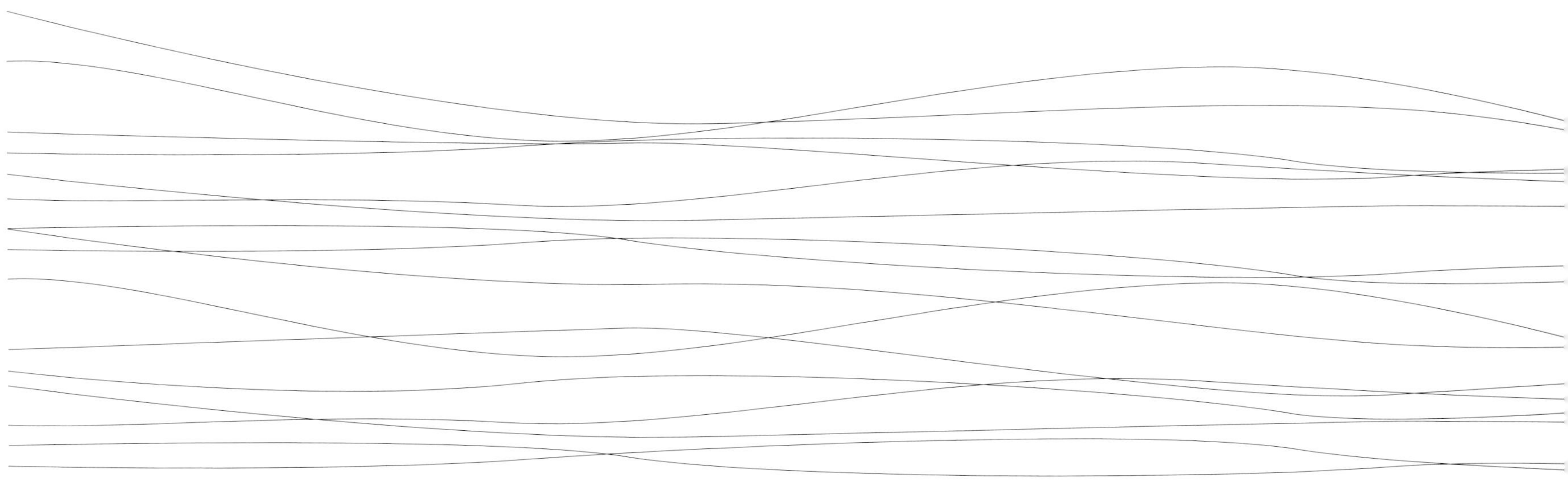

A Prayer of Blue

Japan is at once a modern nation and one steeped in tradition, yet it lacks a strong single religion such as Christianity in the West or Islam in the Arab world. Many Japanese families celebrate Christmas, bury their dead in Buddhist temples, and go to Shinto shrines to welcome in the New Year. In terms of religion, we are a fickle people. The Japanese of old venerated and worshipped all natural objects as deities, and this animistic view is still apparent here. Since ancient times, the Japanese have revered their ancestors' spirits and gods in nature. This was in turn informed by foreign philosophies, such as Buddhism, Confucianism, or Taoism, and formalized as Shintoism. The propensity of Japanese people to believe that all things in the natural world have a soul or spiritual presence may be viewed as an influence of Shintoism.

When I saw the photographs taken by Lucille Reyboz in Japan, at first I felt that she was looking to find an animistic style of supernaturalism within Japanese people. I have already mentioned the curious coexistence of state-of-the-art technology and primeval spiritual perceptions in Japan; without falling into the silver-screen clichés of geishas and hara-kiri-committing samurais that are in vogue today, she has instead carefully captured the sense of spiritual prayer and healing carried over from the time of Himiko, queen regnant of the legendary realm of Yamatai in the third century.

This collection of works takes as its setting Japan's hot springs and modern bathhouses with their links to animism. While spa areas in Europe are usually geared toward drinking water, in Japan they are primarily for bathing. Generally known as *onsen*, they also offer food and accommodation. For the Japanese, *onsen* represent a haven of rest for both body and soul, and are found throughout the country; Lucille attempts to liken Mother Earth's hot mineral spring water to the womb. The fact that *onsen* are dotted all over the nation is due to the high level of seismic events in the Japanese archipelago—a zone prone to frequent earthquakes and volcanic activity—and this is not unrelated to animistic beliefs enduring from ancient times. Lucille's focus on *onsen* is founded on this insight.

Glancing through the works, I felt a sense of incongruity in the studied compositions, but soon came to realize that it is the technology employed in these very compositions that has brought out a particularly Japanese style of beauty. They exuded for me a subtle but quintessentially Japanese rhythm. In her quest for animism, Japan's beauty aside, Lucille has sought to portray the solitude, isolation, strife, reconciliation, future, symbolic value, surface, and depths of Japan (and the Japanese). It is indeed impressive how the photographer's own battle rises like a prayer from within each photograph's calm and tranquil blueness.

Lucille's previous works include a collection of photographs taken of a tribe living in a "non-civilized" African society. One of these photographs shows a newborn baby emerging through a round hole in the wall of a mud hut, evocative of the mouth of the womb. The Japanese *onsen* may indeed be the womb beyond this hole. I was pleasantly overwhelmed by her ability and critical sensibility as a photographer in her exquisite comparison of the lives of African people and the animistic perceptions of the cyber-Japanese; the former remain close to their primeval roots, while the latter quickly threw off their primeval roots to wallow shoulder-deep in the tepid waters of technological civilization.

In one of the photographs, the wet tresses of a raven-haired woman stream like lava from out of the darkness; it might be the strongest expression of the excitement Lucille must have felt gazing at a quintessentially Japanese universe. To me, a Japanese man living in Paris, this was very much like the spiritual incarnation of another Japan, the one I see when I look back at my homeland.

Hitonari Tsuji

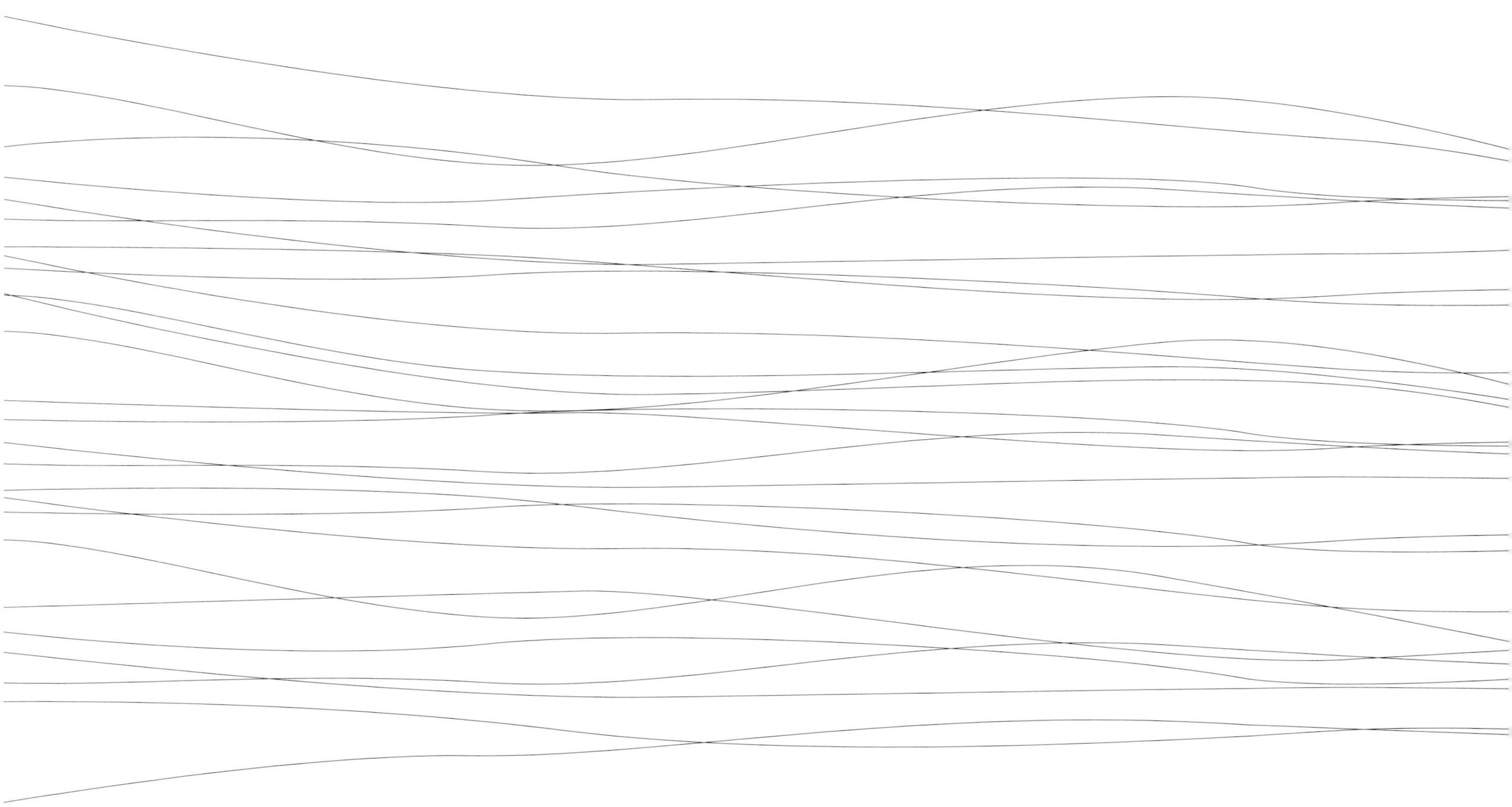

青の祈り

そういえば、日本という国はこれほど伝統があり、しかも近代国家でありながら、同時に西洋におけるキリスト教やアラブ諸国におけるイスラム教のごとき強い単一の宗教を持たない。多くの日本人はクリスマスを祝い、死者は寺で葬られ、正月には神社に初詣に出掛ける。宗教的に見れば節操のない民族にも映る。ここにはあらゆる自然物を神として崇め奉った太古の日本人のアニミズム観が影響を与えている。古来から日本人は祖先神や自然神への尊崇を持っており、これが外来思想である仏教や儒教、道教などの影響を受けて神道として理論化されることになった。日本人が自然界のあらゆる事物の中に精霊や霊的存在を認めようとするのは、神道の影響ということも出来るだろう。

Lucille Reyboz の日本で撮影された幾つかの作品を見た時、まず最初に、彼女が日本人の中に、アニミズム的超自然観を見つけようとしていることを感じた。日本の最先端のテクノロジーと原初的アニミズム世界観の奇妙な同居がここでは語られているが、昨今流行りの、サムライ芸者ハラキリのサユリ的勘違い日本批評には陥っておらず、むしろそこには丁寧に、三世紀に邪馬台国を率いた女帝、卑弥呼の時代から受け継がれてきた霊的な祈りと癒しのあり方が切り取られていた。

作品集は日本の温泉場、並びに温泉的なアニミズムとリンクする形の近代的な浴場を舞台に作られている。日本の温泉場は欧州でよく見かける飲用としての温泉場とは異なり、主に、浴用として活用され、そこに宿や食事所などが併設され、総称して温泉と呼ばれている。日本人の精神と肉体の休息の場として、全国的に広まったが、ルシールはこの内部からあふれ出る熱い鉱泉の温泉場を日本女性の子宮になぞらえようとしている。日本全国に温泉が分布しているのは、日本がプレート・テクトニクス学的にいって、地震多発地帯、並びに火山活動の中心地に位置する島国であるからで、これらのことは古代から続く日本のアニミズム信仰と無縁ではない。ルシールが温泉に着目したのは、このような洞察に基づくものであろう。

作品を一瞥した時、計算され尽くした構図に違和感を覚えたが、まもなく、この構図こそが彼女が描こうとしているテクノロジー日本の様式美を現しているものだ、と理解することが出来た。構図の中に緻密だが土着的なリズムを感じたのである。アニミズムを見つめようとしながら、Lucille は日本の美だけに係わらず、日本（人）の孤独、孤立、確執、和解、未来、象徴、表層、深層を描こうとしていた。その写真家としての格闘する姿が、静謐な青色の写真の内側から祈りとともに浮き上がっていたのが実に印象的であった。

前作、アフリカの非文明社会に生きる一部族を撮影した写真集の中に、土の家の寝室に通じる子宮口のような丸い穴から、産まれたばかりの赤ん坊がまさに出ようとしている写真があった。日本の温泉はまさにその穴の先の子宮なのであろう。原始をそのまま引き受けて生きるアフリカ人の生活と、原始をいち早く脱ぎ捨ててテクノロジー文明のぬるま湯に肩まで浸かりきった電脳日本人のアニミズム観とを絶妙に比較する彼女の写真家としての批評性と力量に、私は心地よく身を任せることが出来た。

闇の中から、黒髪の女性の濡れた無数の髪が溶岩のように広がる一枚の写真の中に、私はもっとも強く、彼女が興奮して見つめてきたに違いない日本的な精神世界の特異性を見させてもらえた気がした。それはパリで生きる日本人である私が、この数年、祖国を振り返る時につい見つめてしまう、もう一つの日本の霊的な姿に酷似していた。

辻仁成

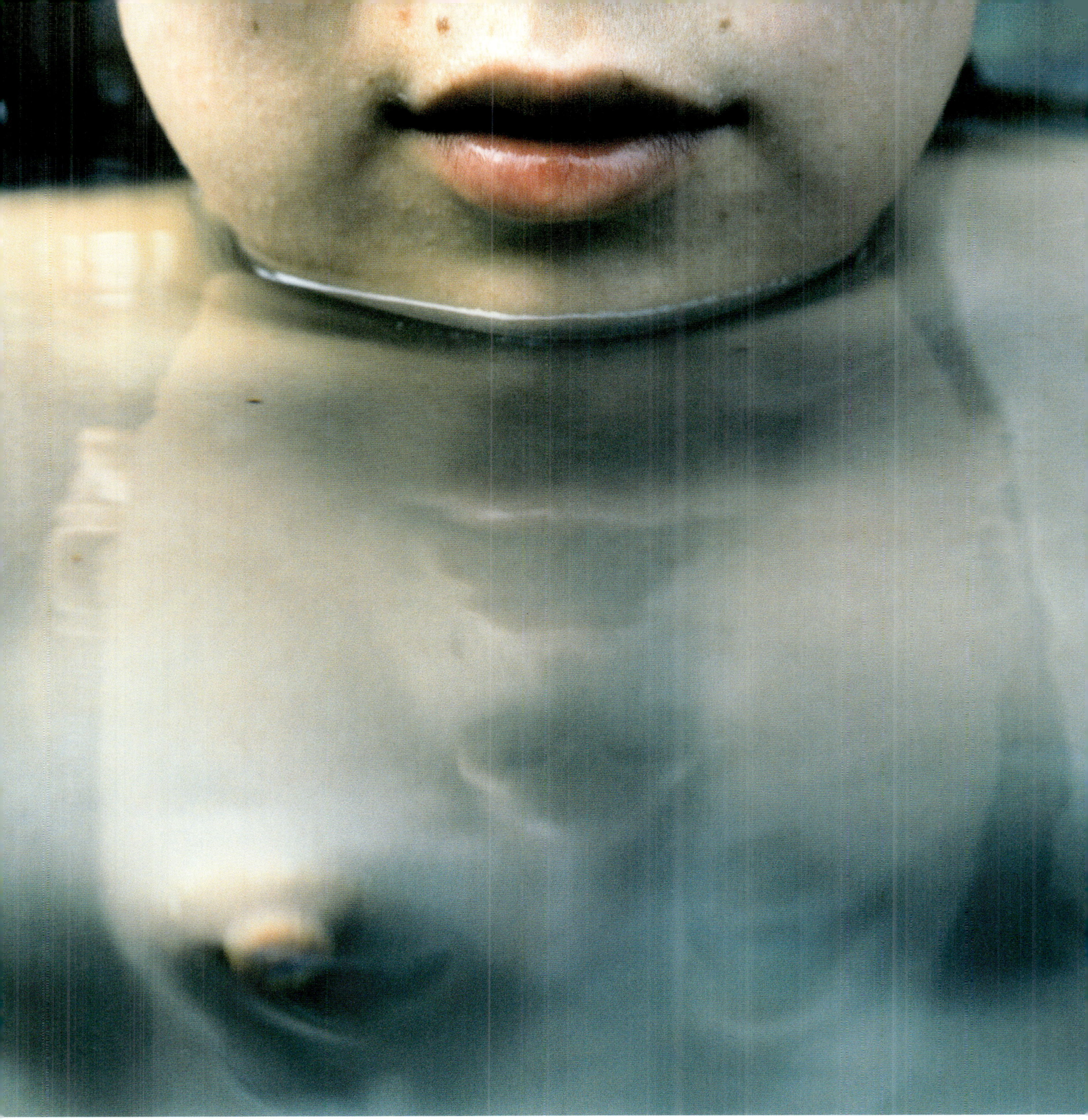

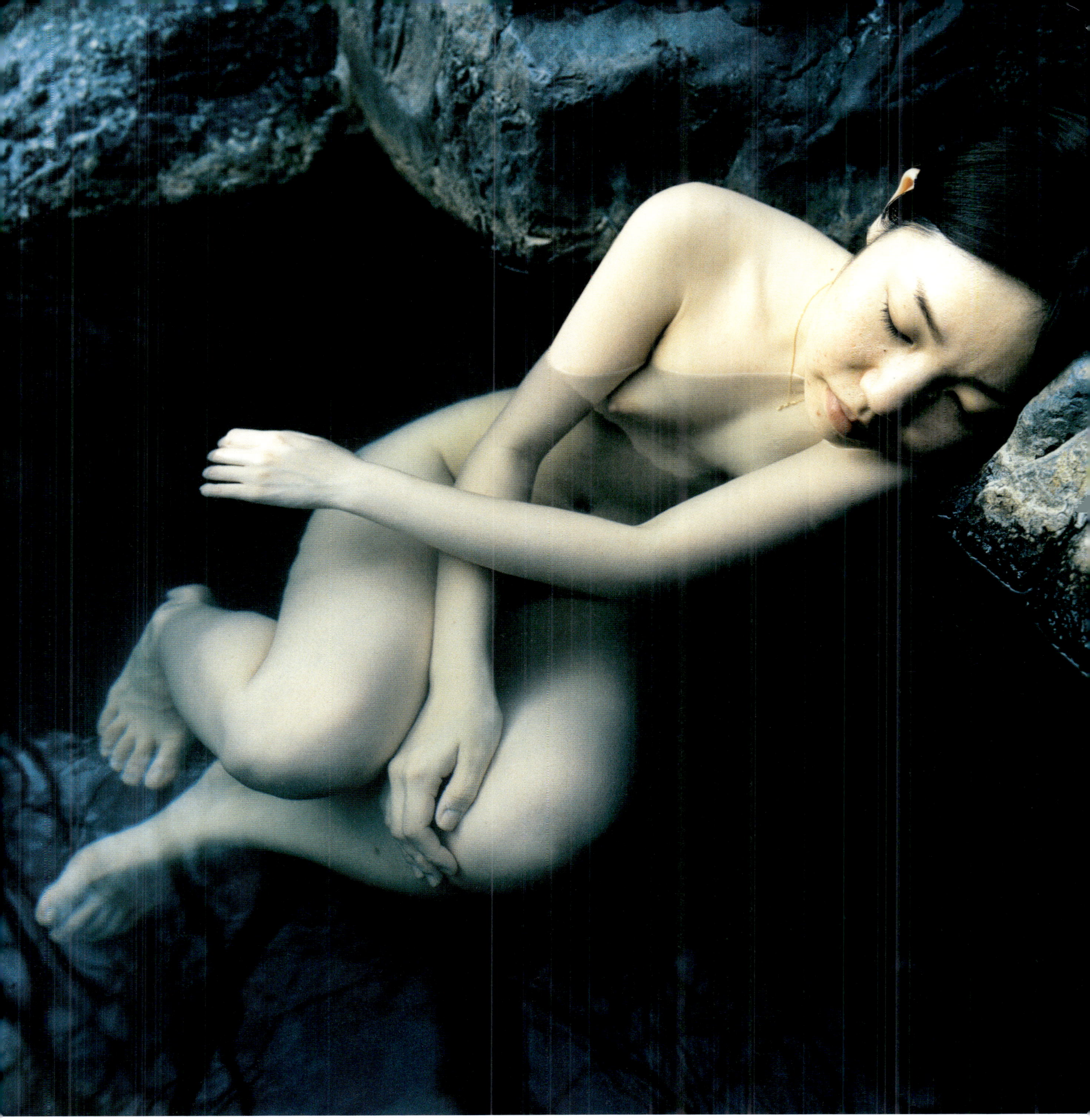

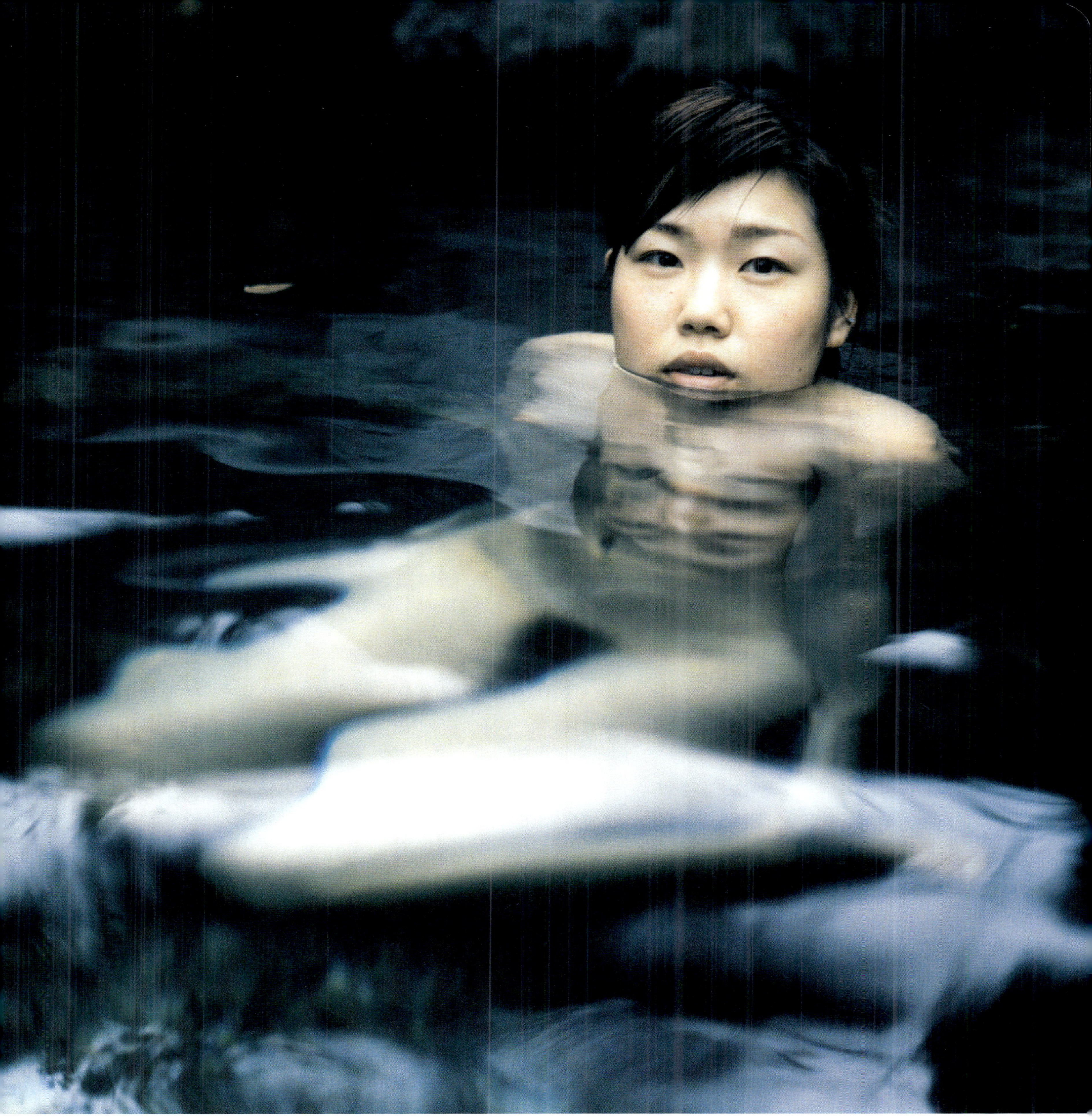

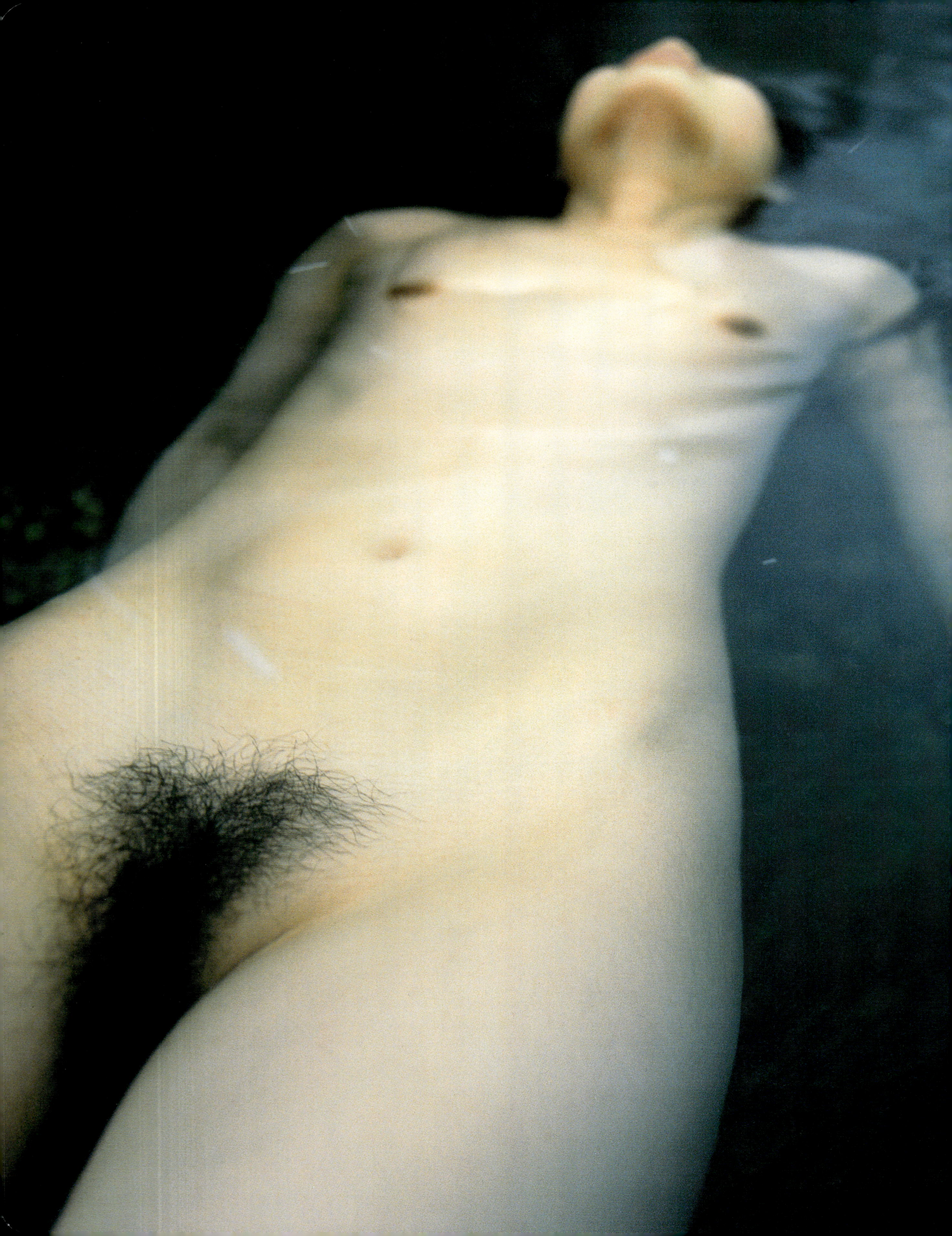

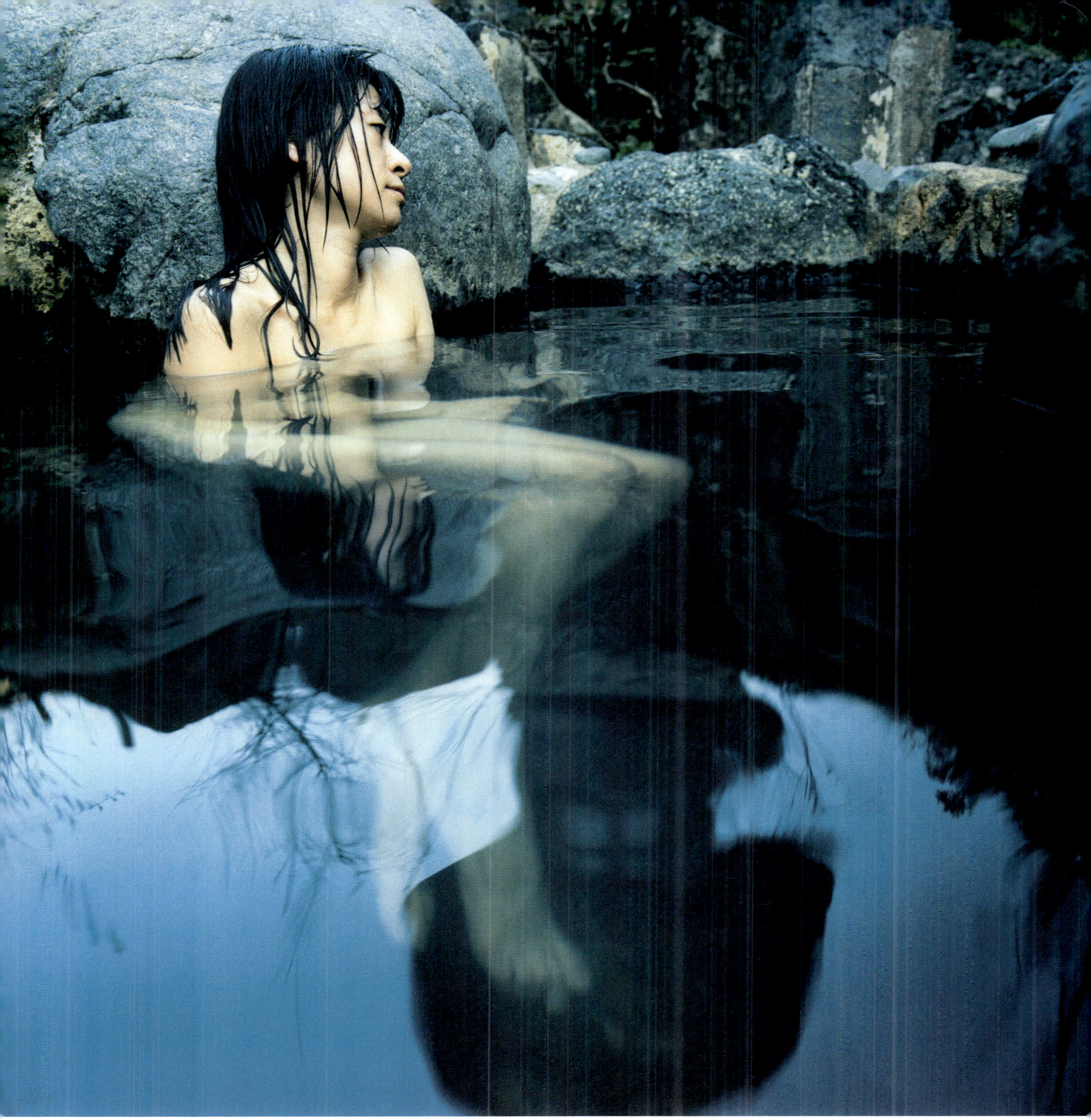

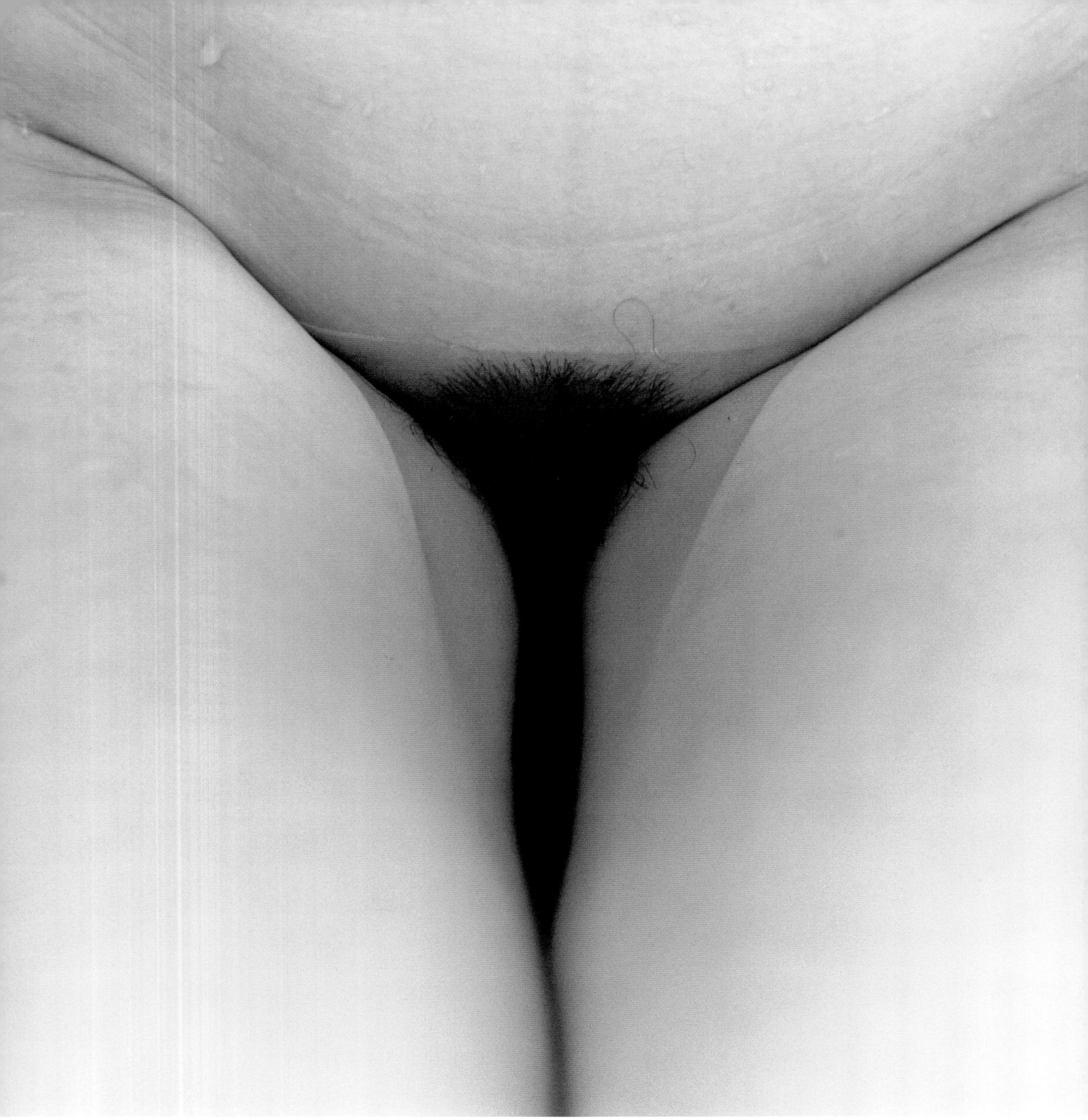

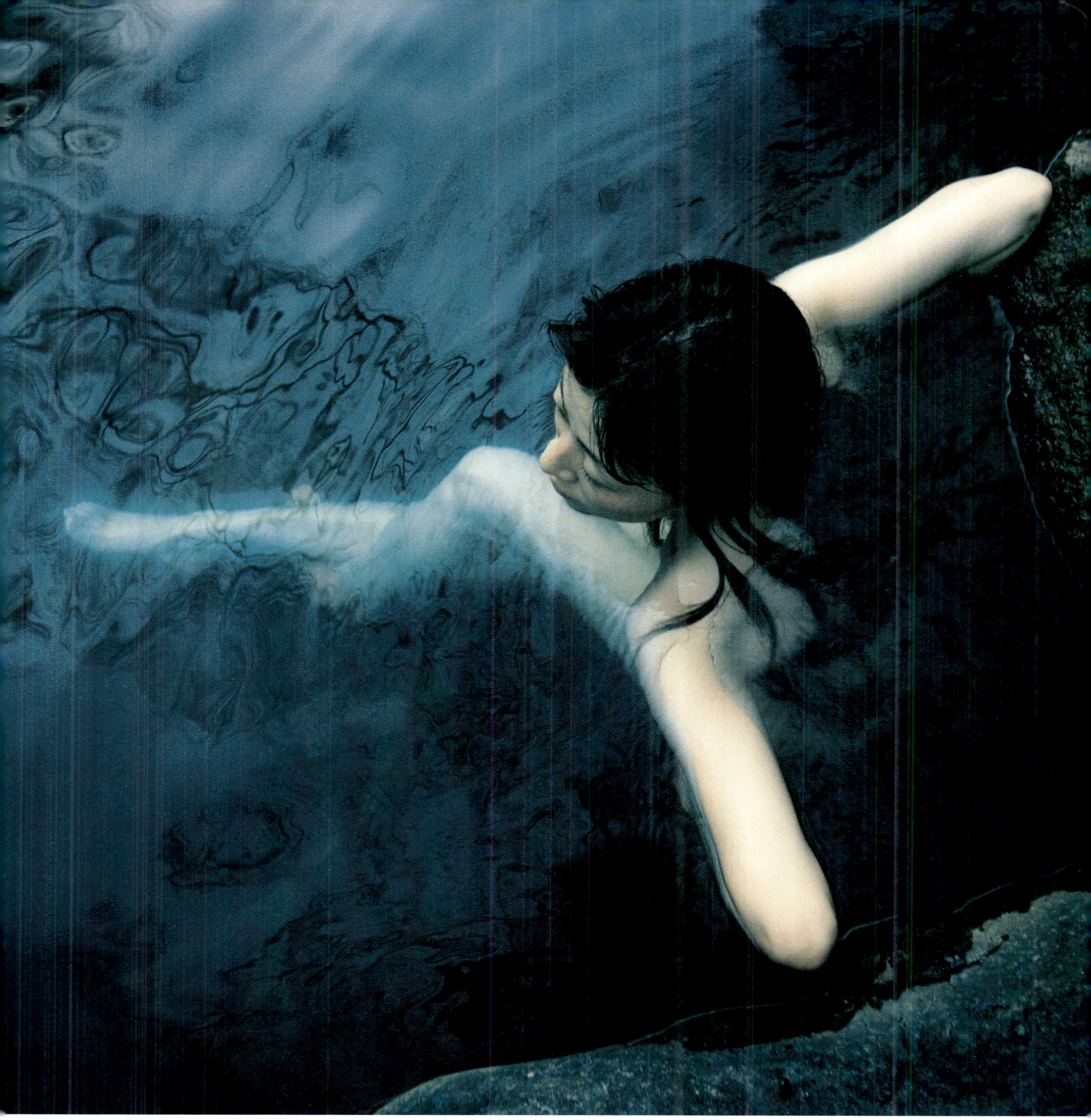

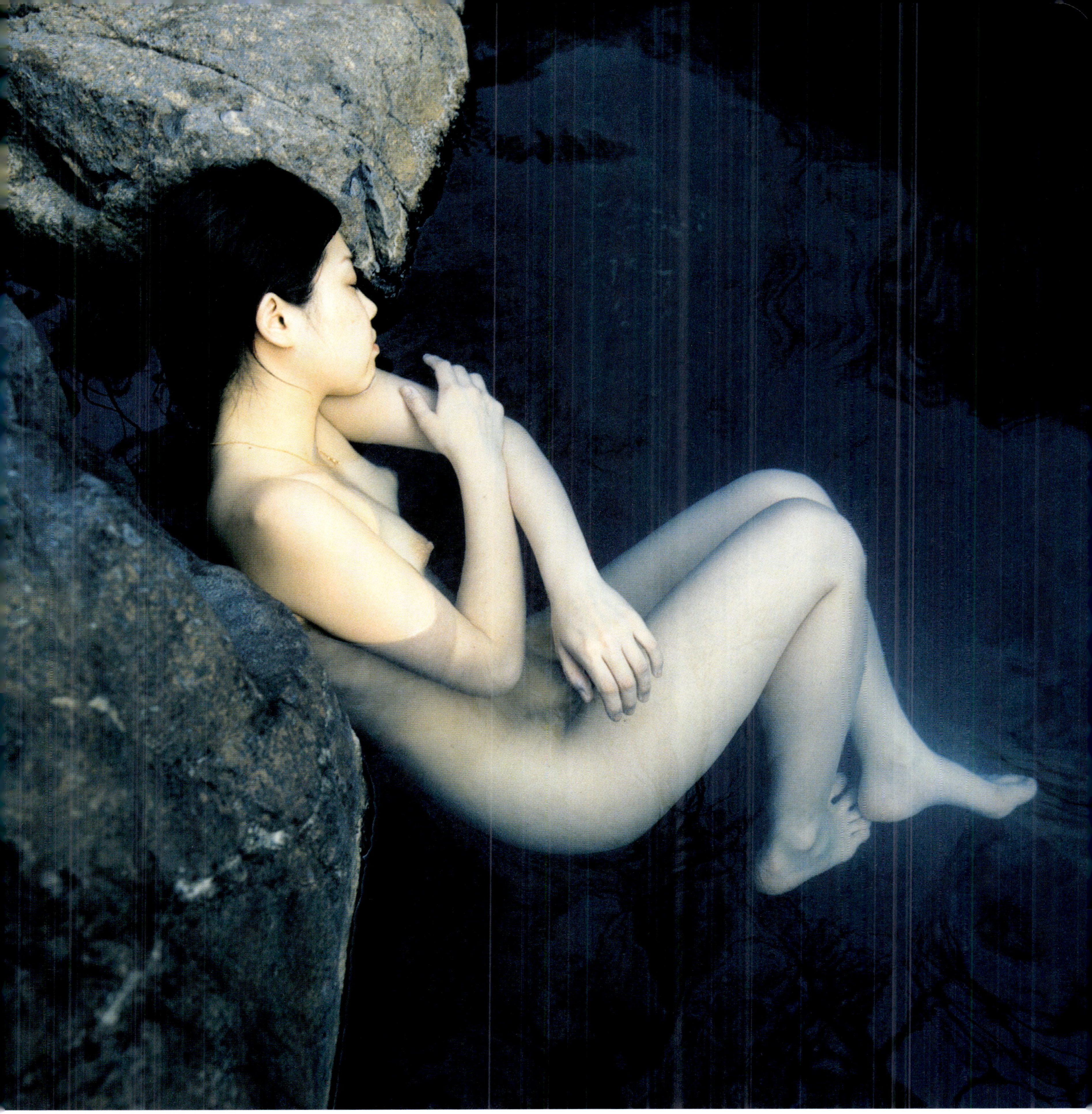

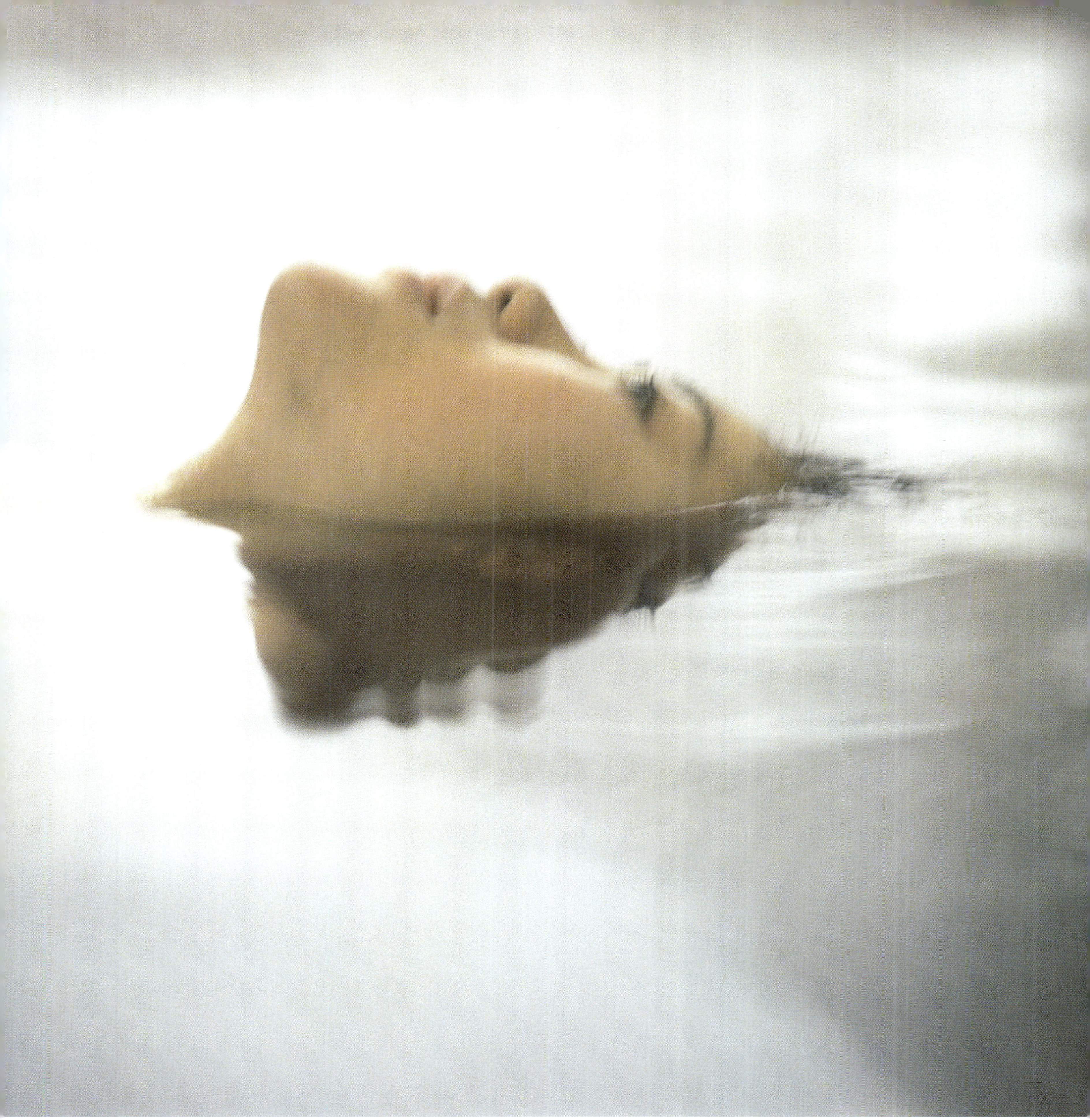

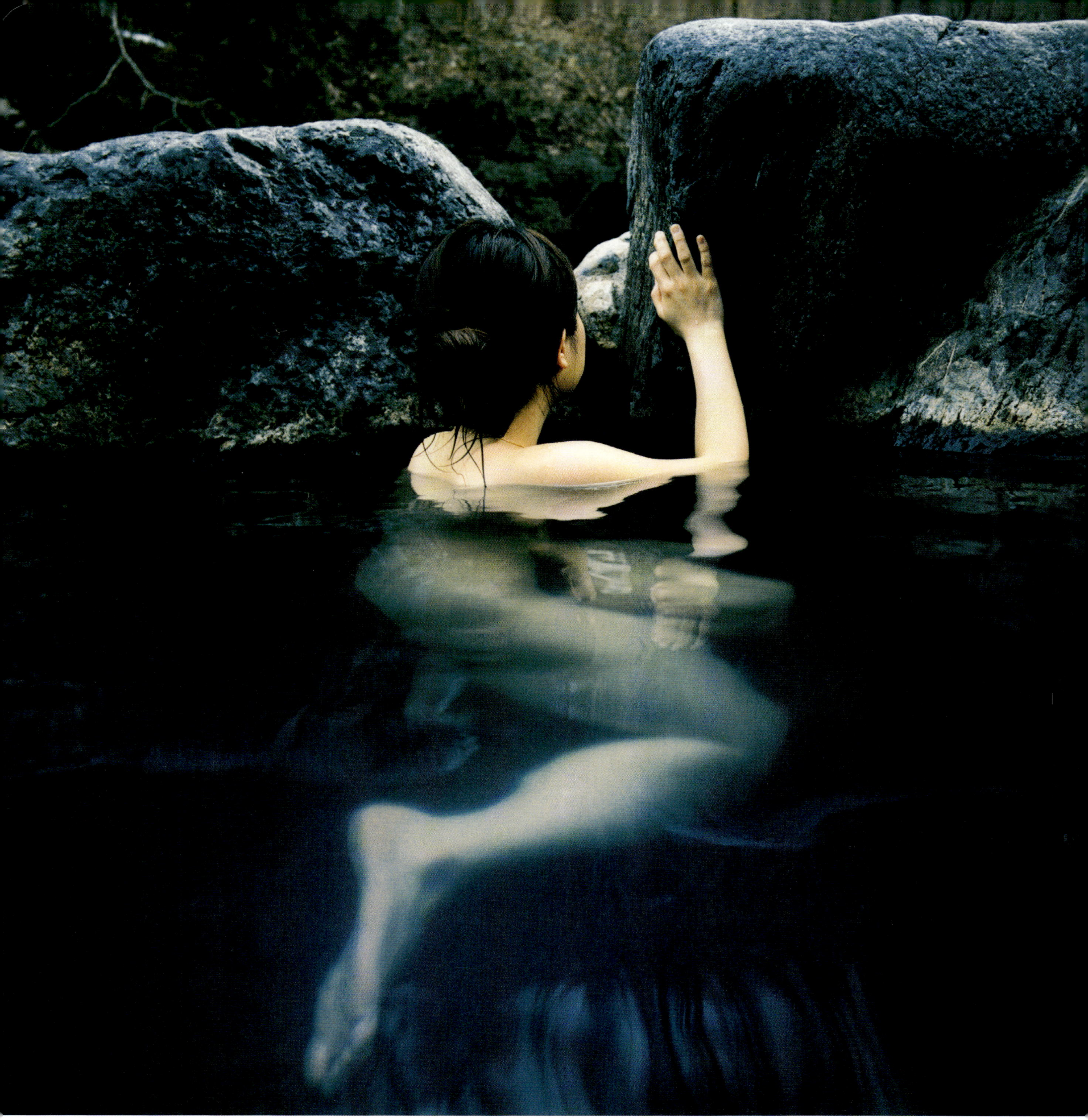

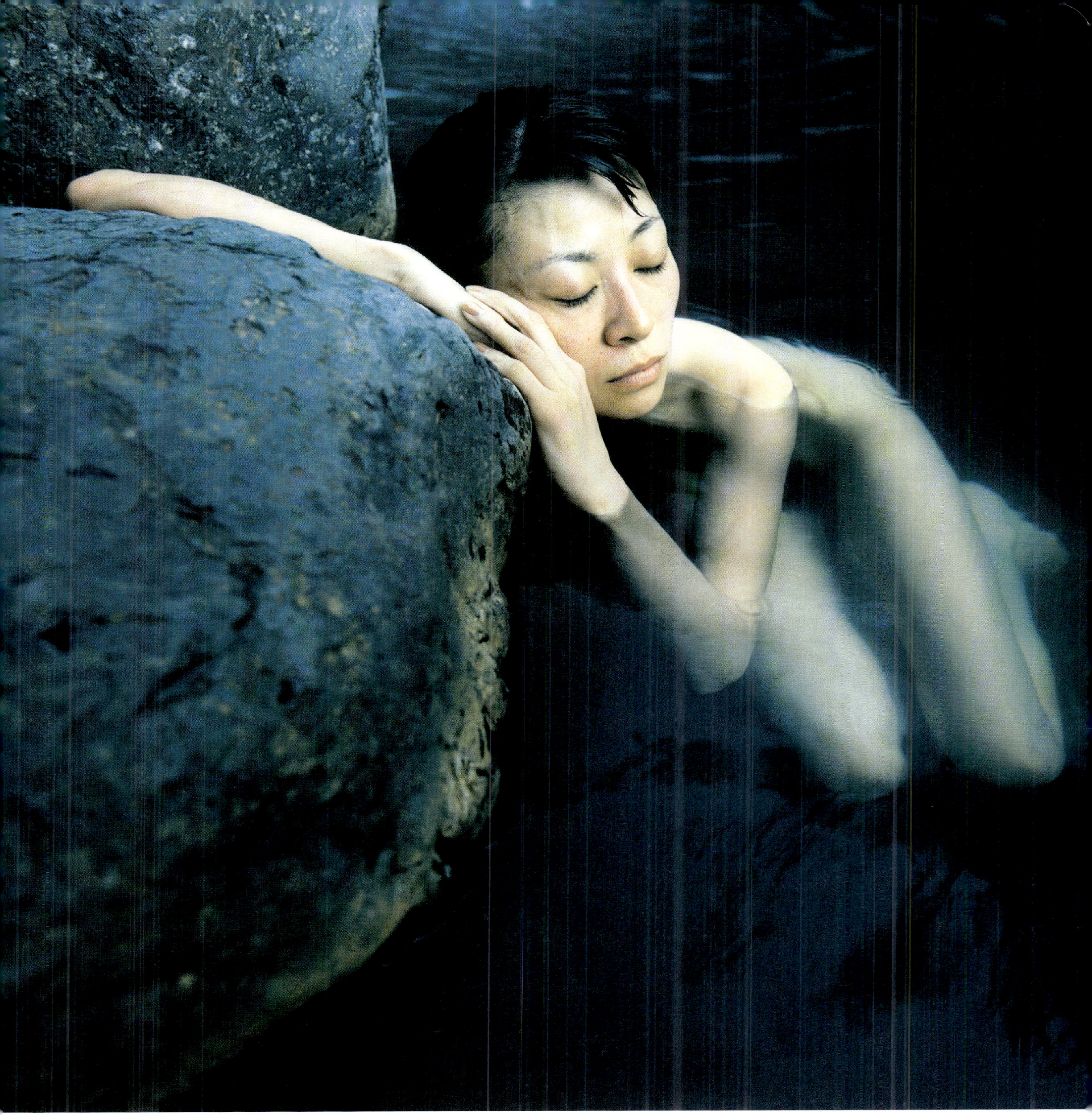

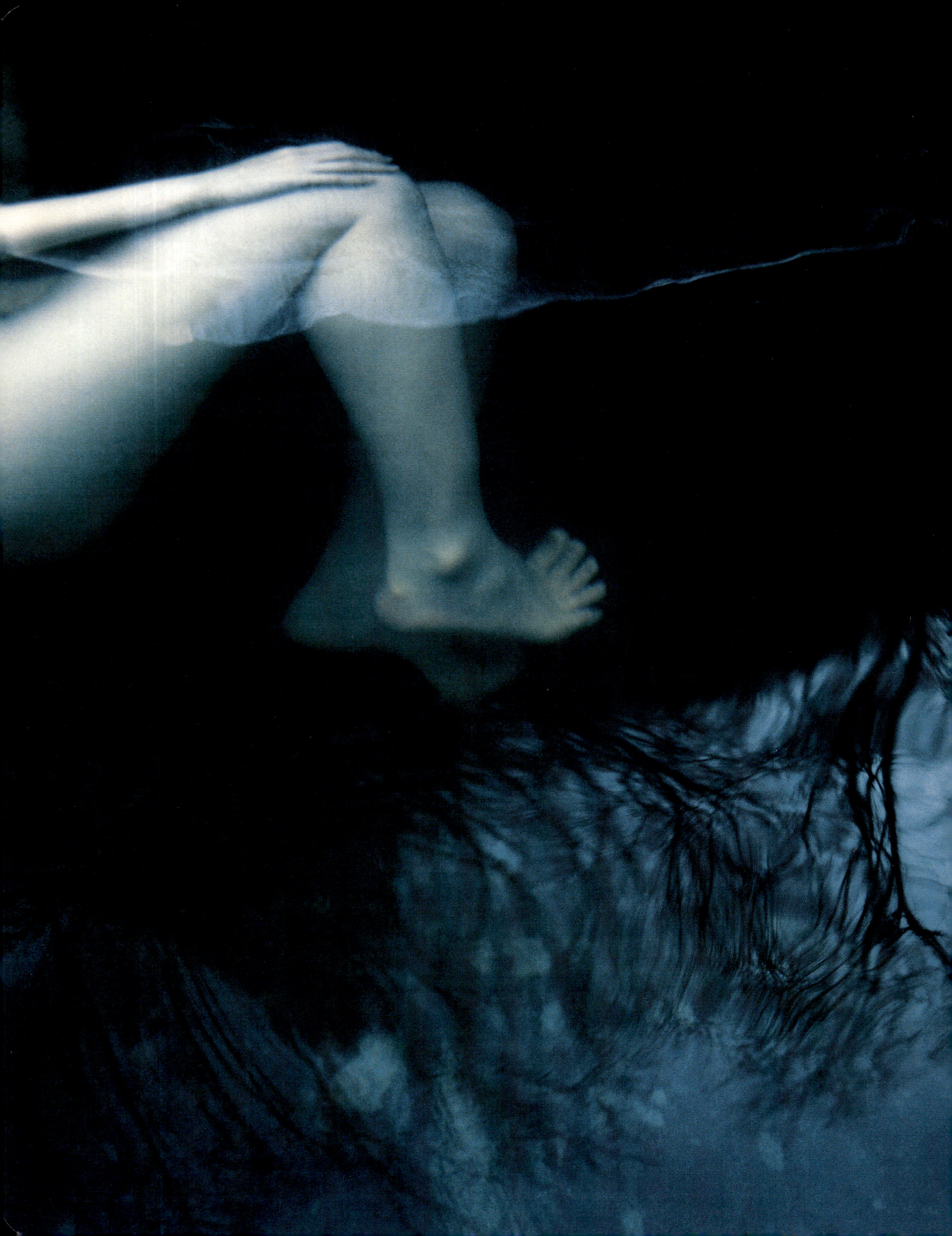

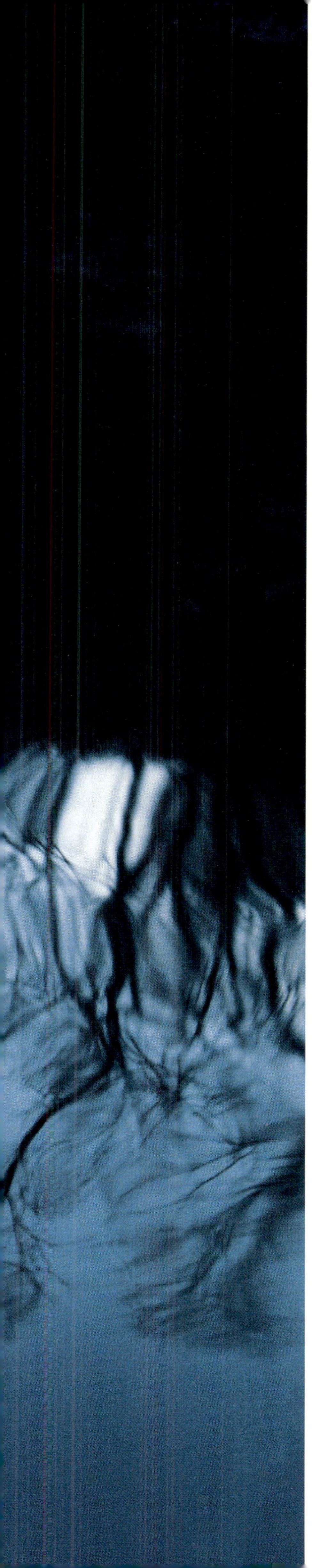

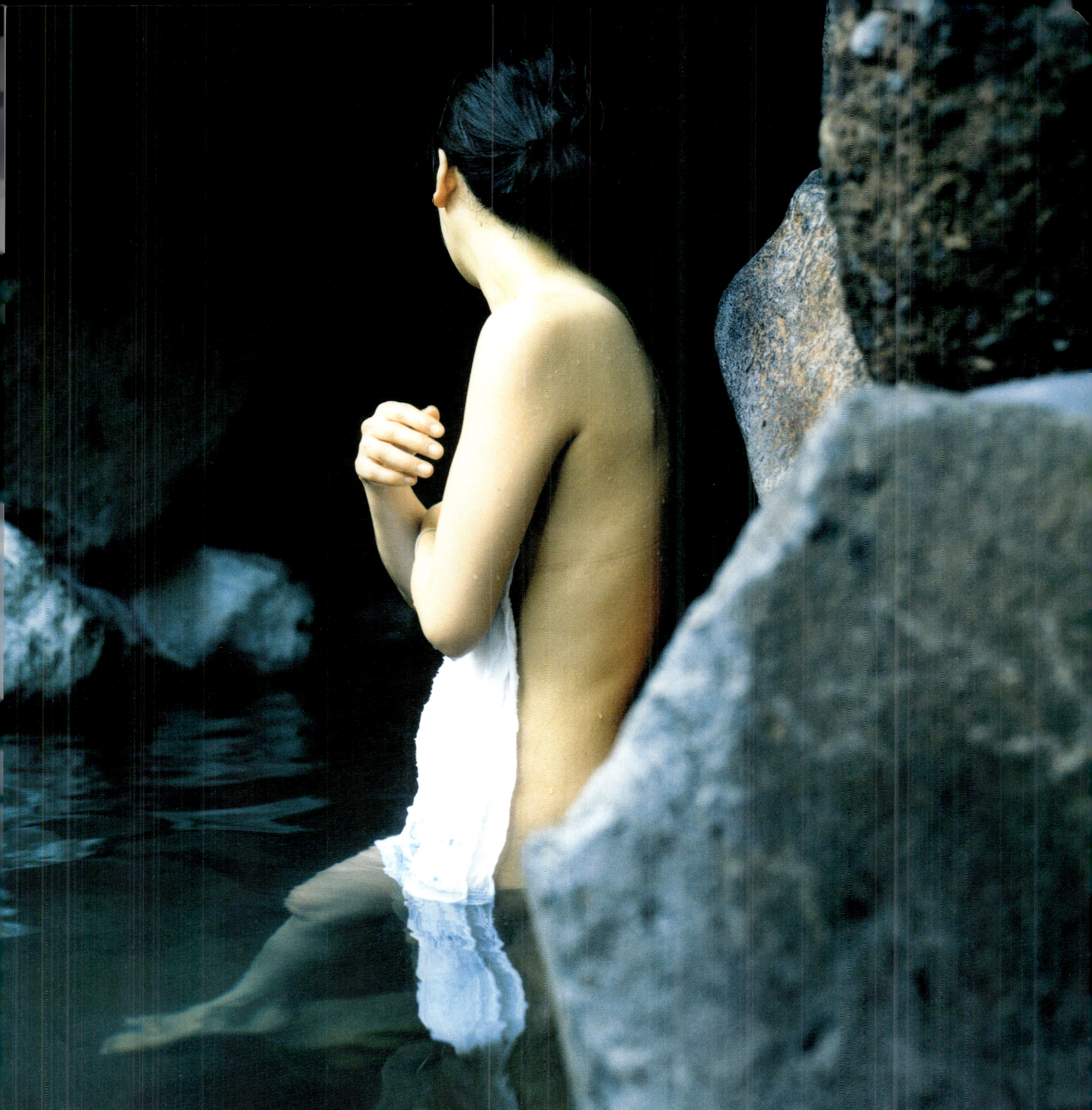

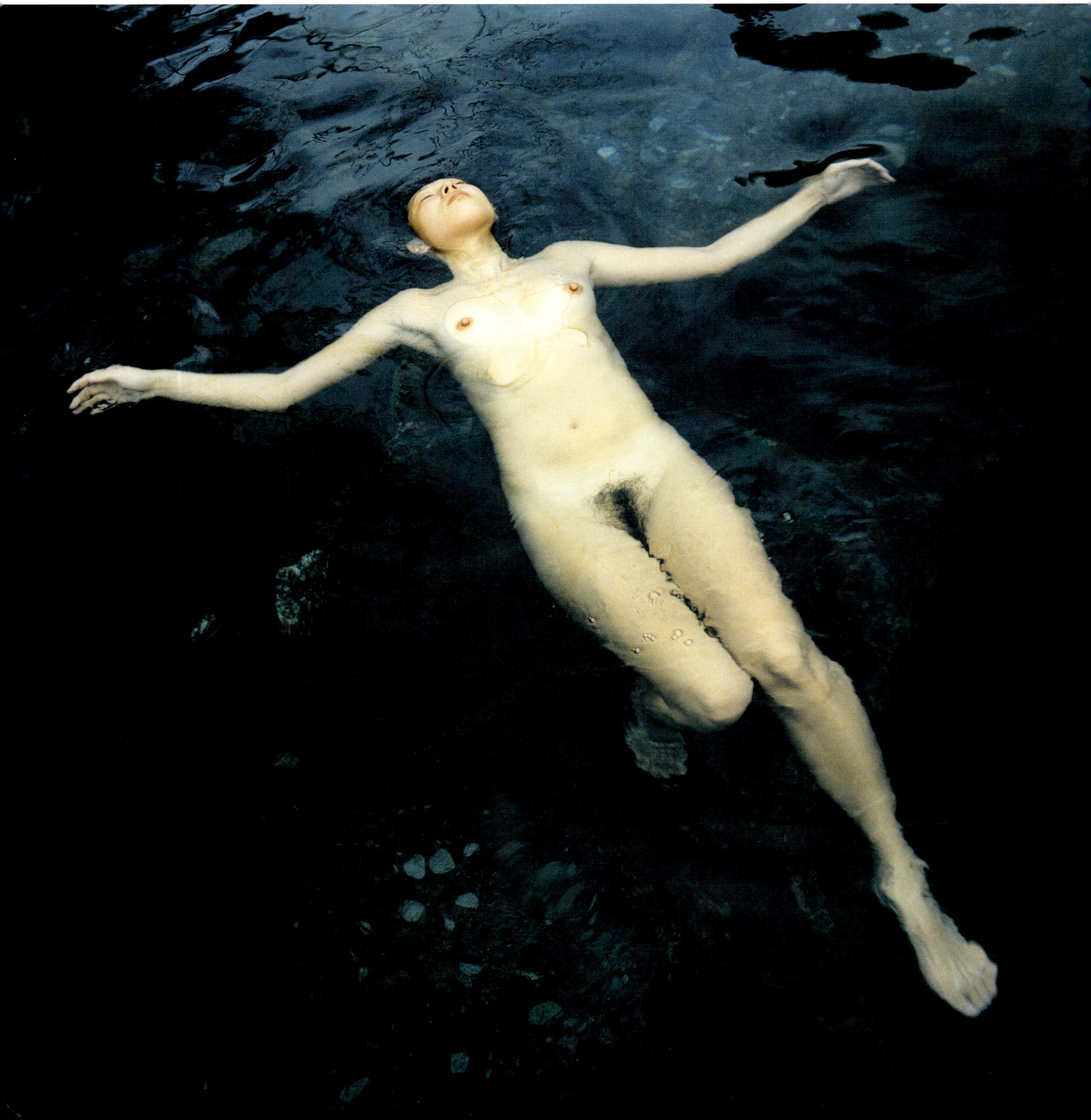

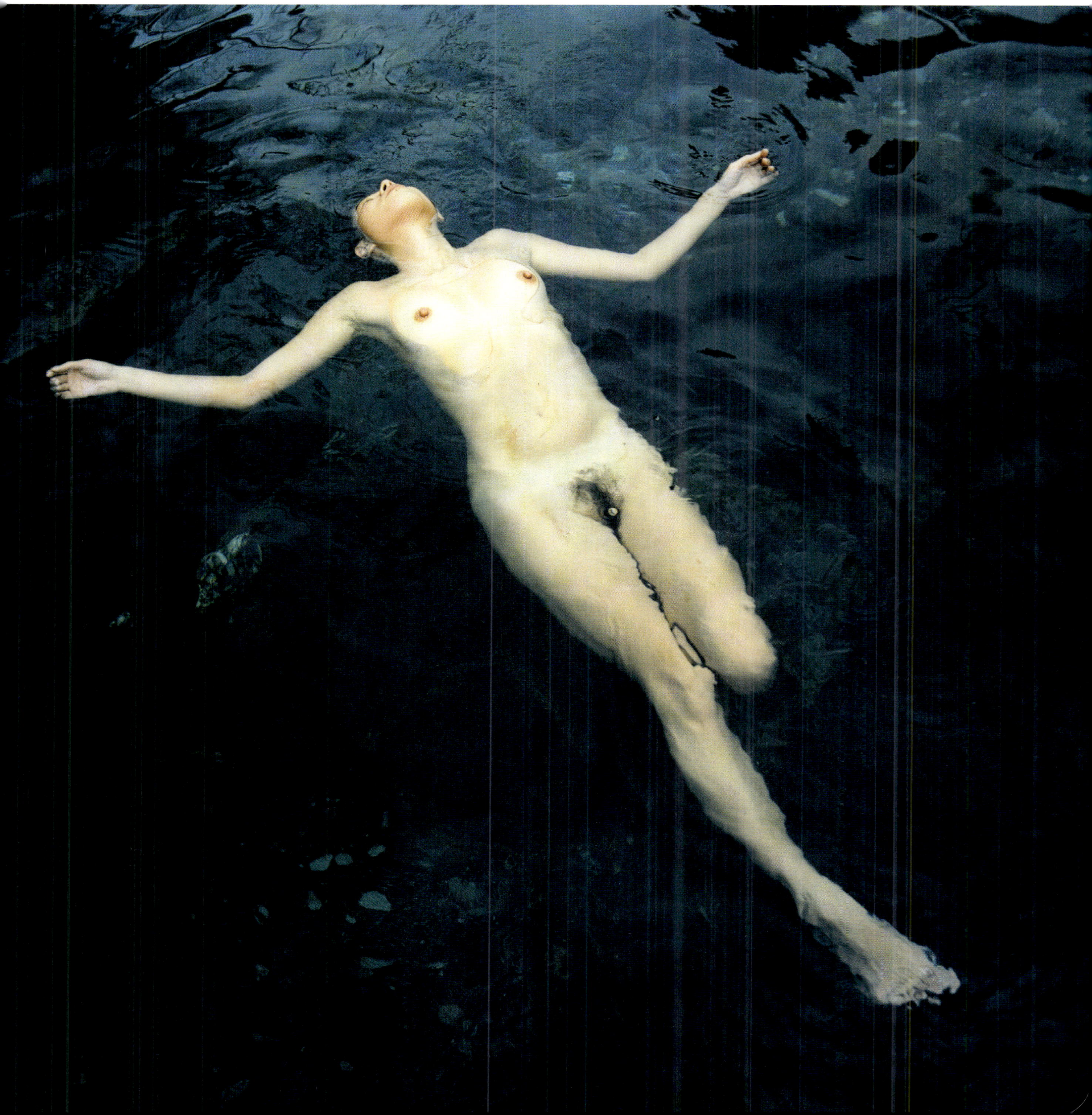

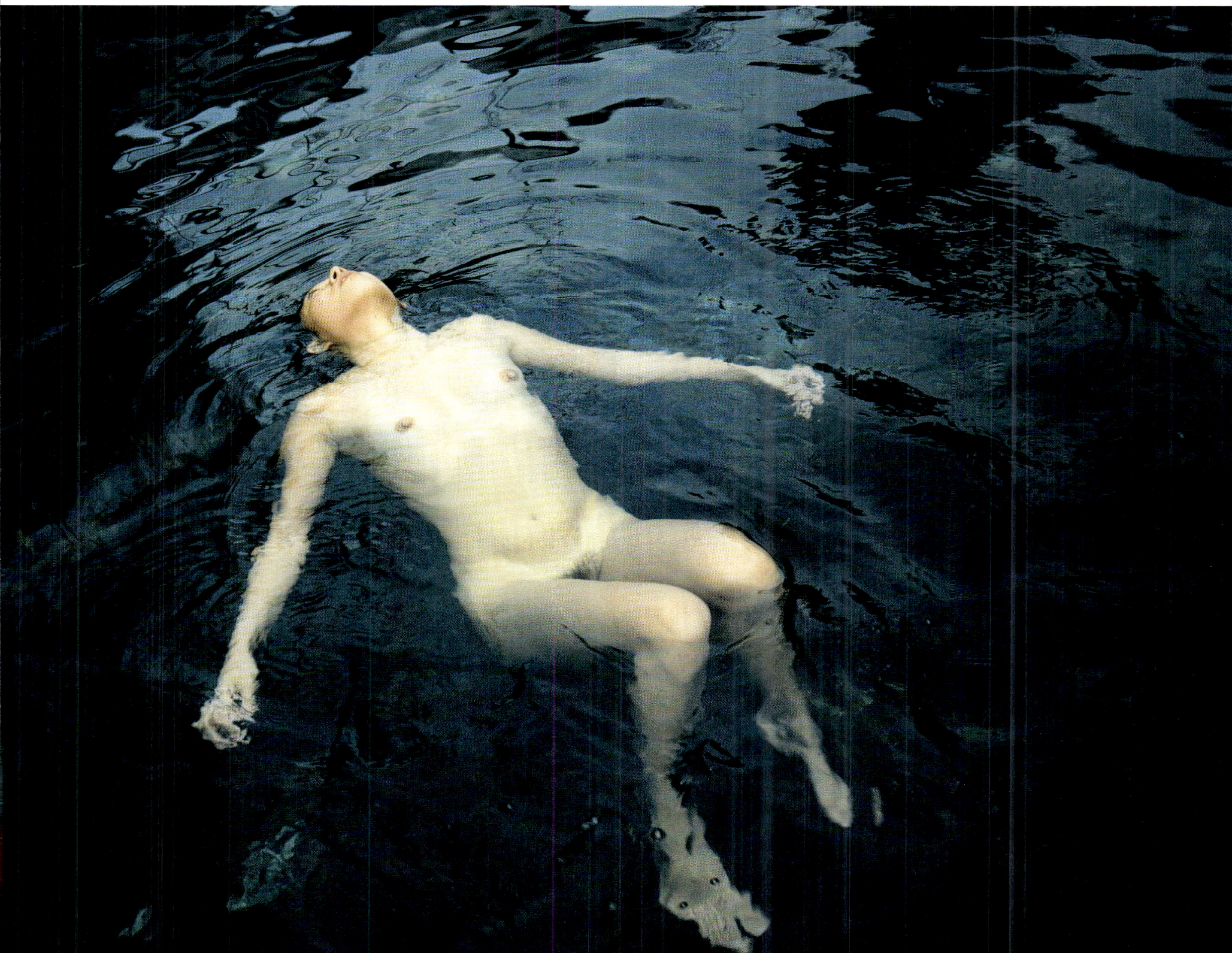

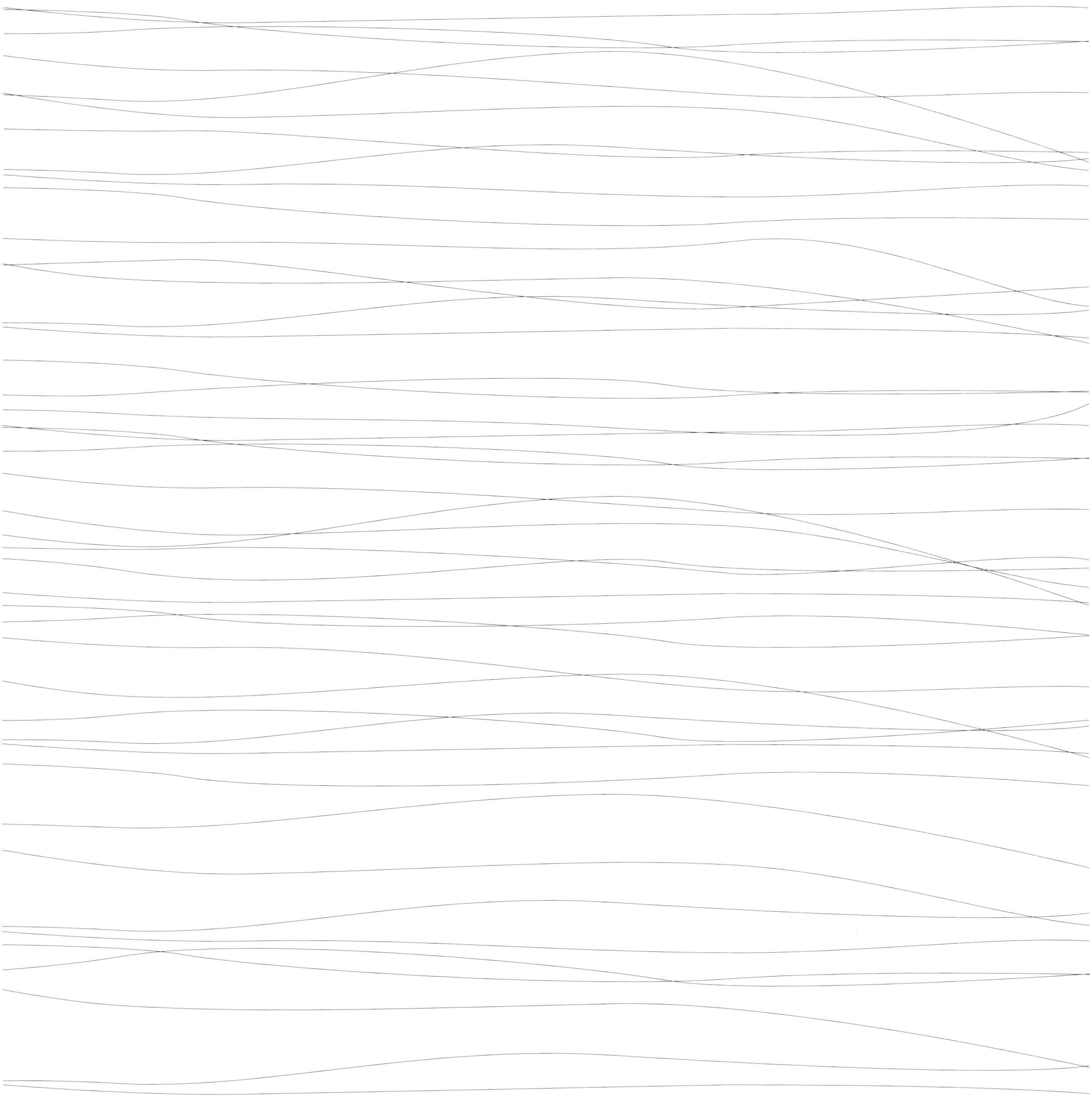

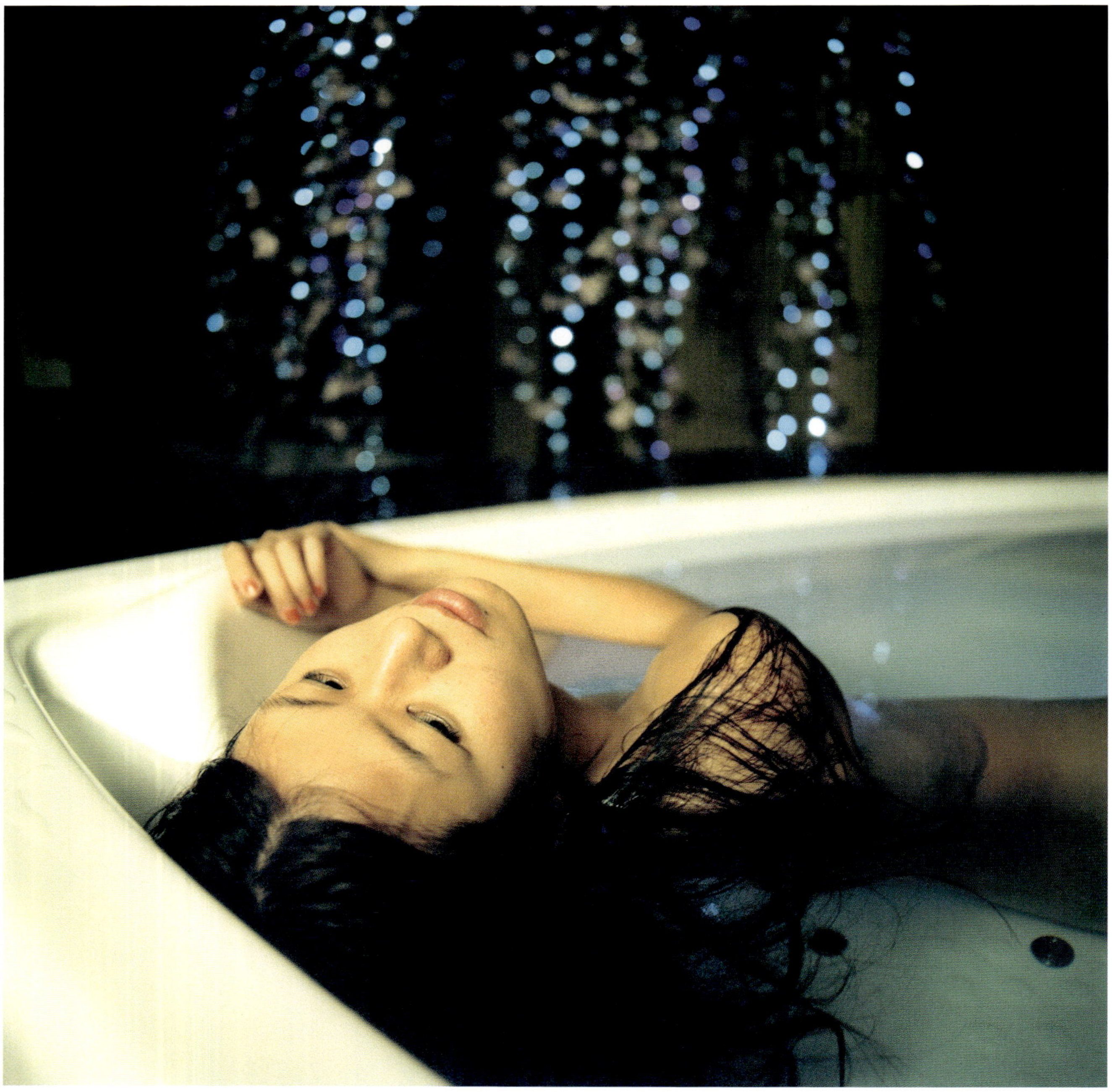

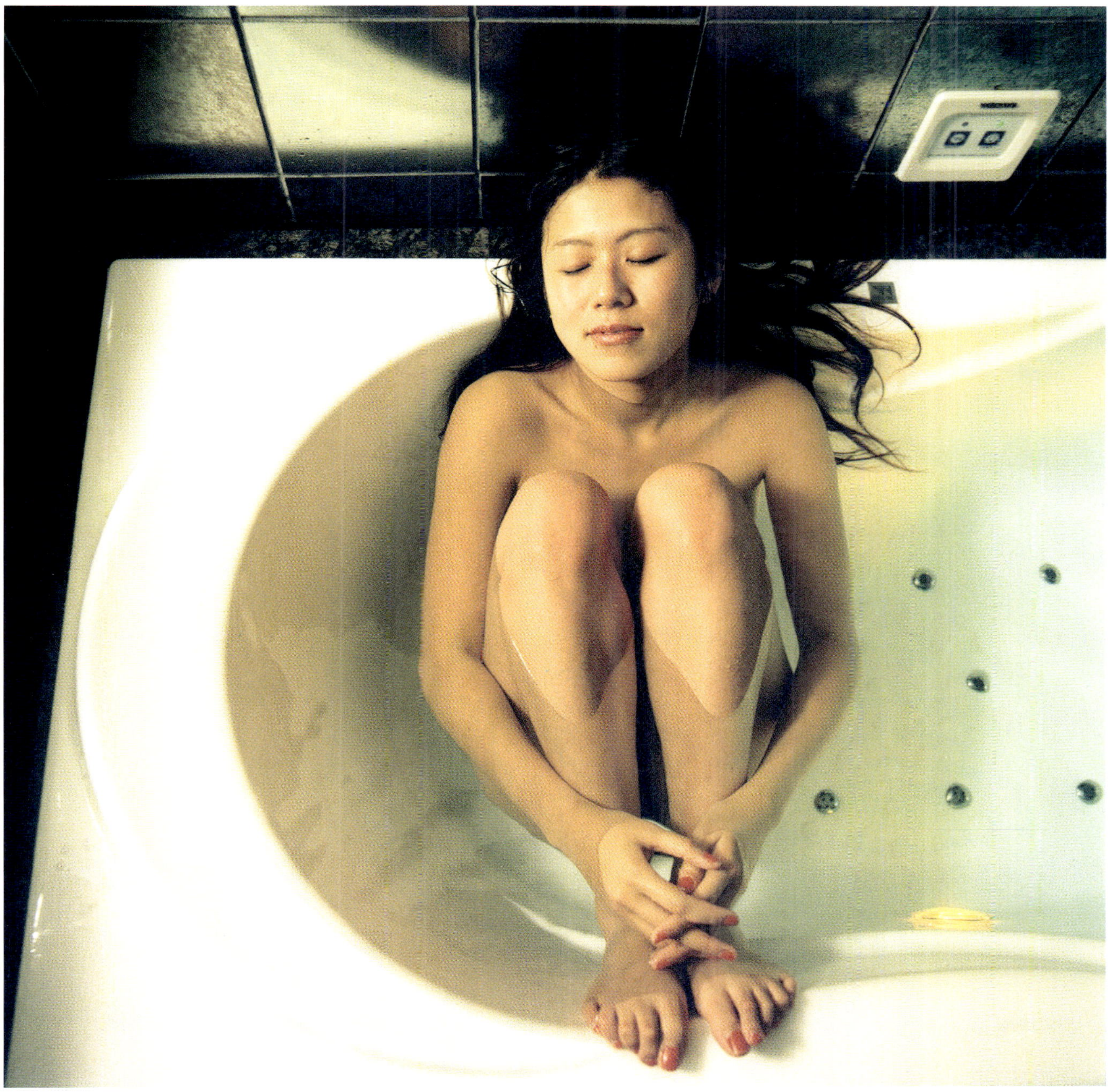

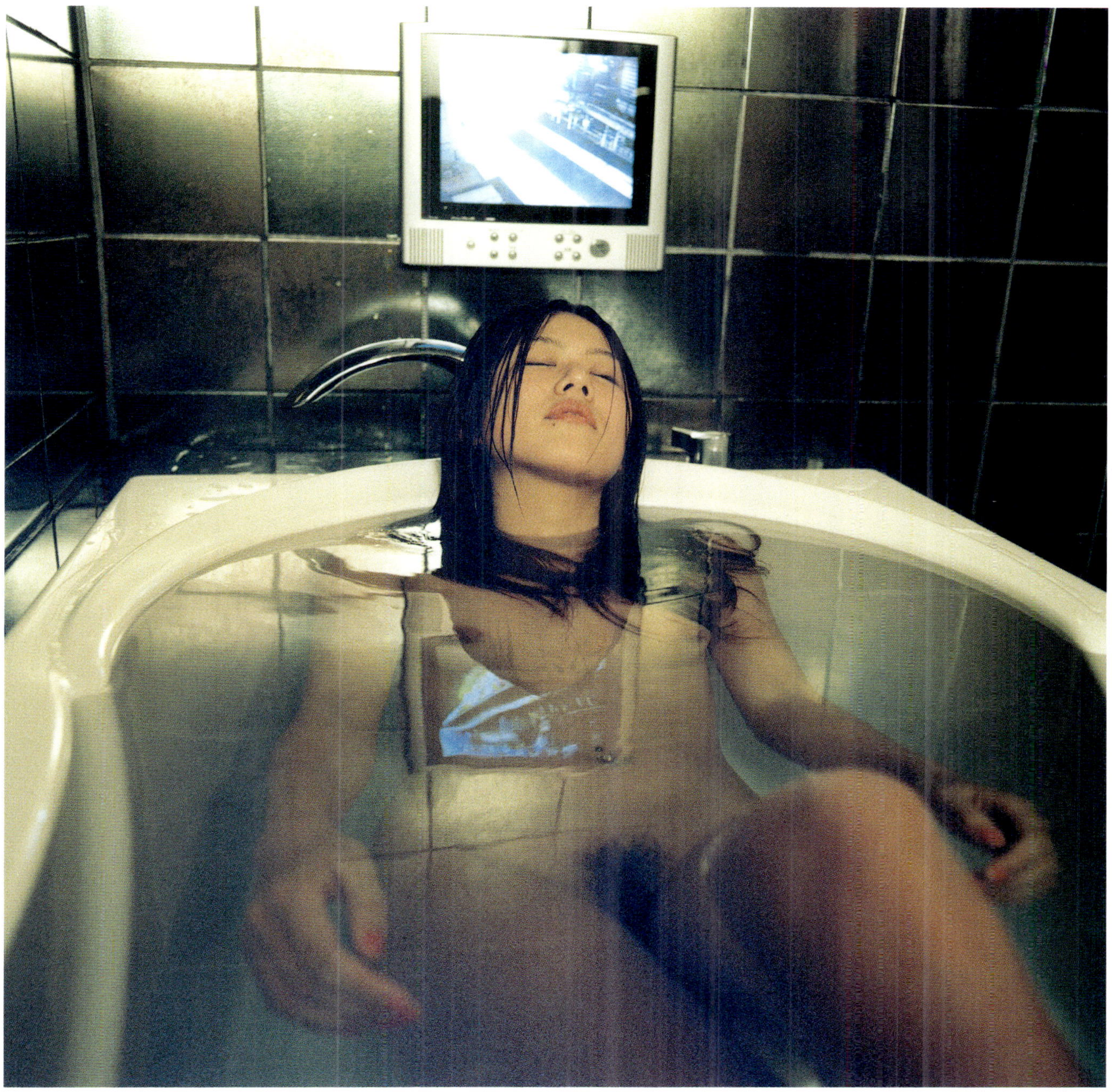

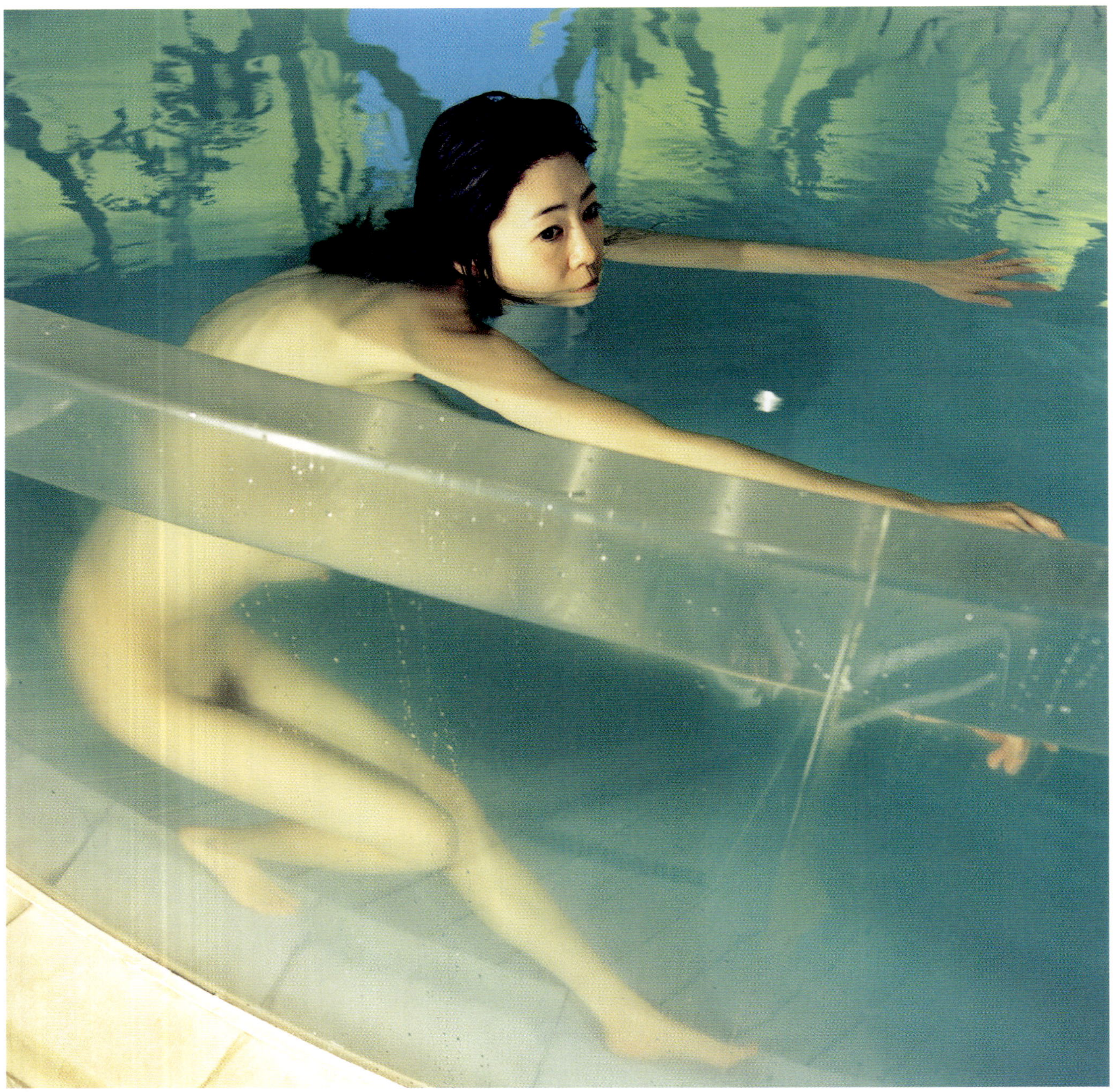

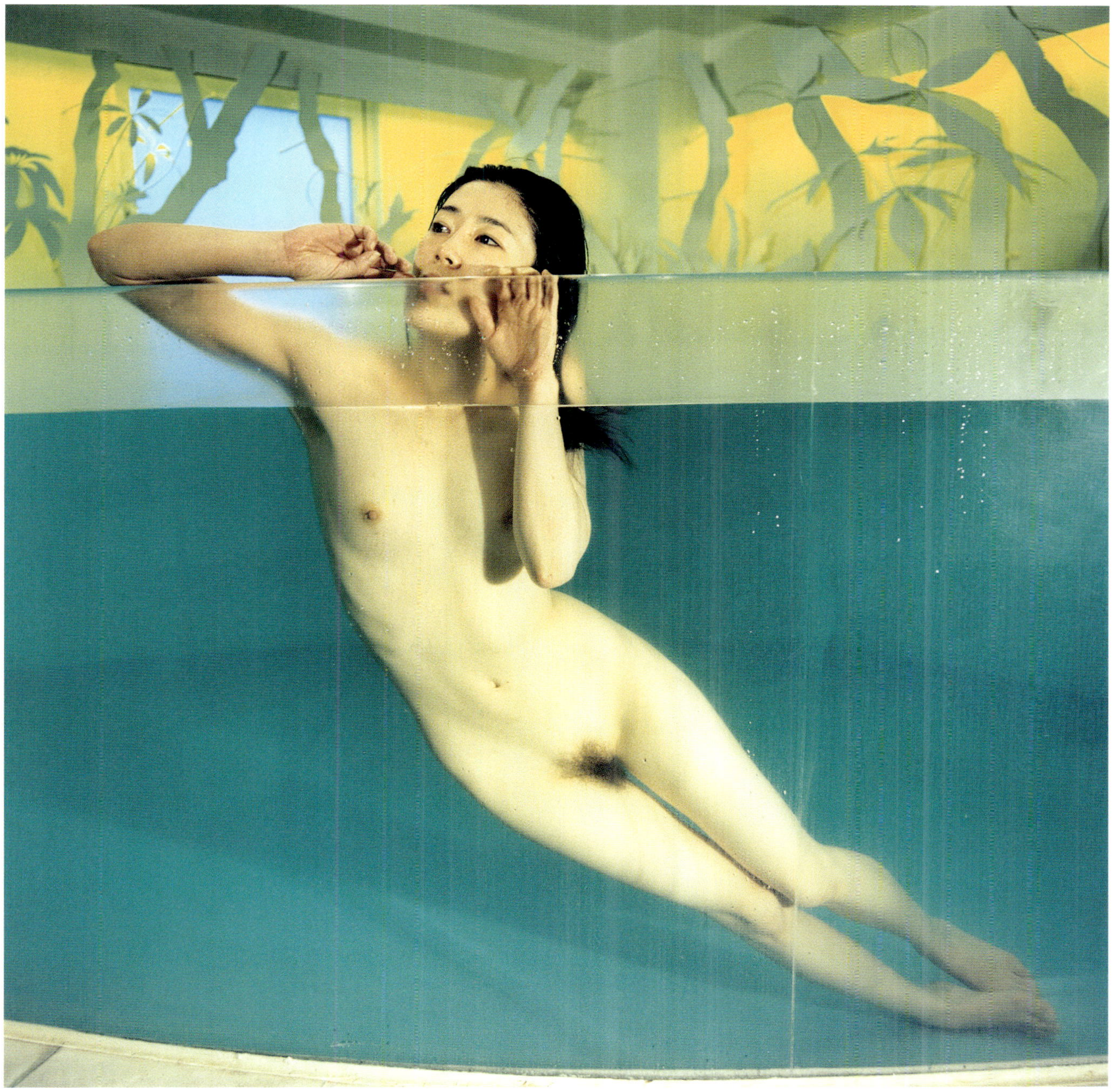

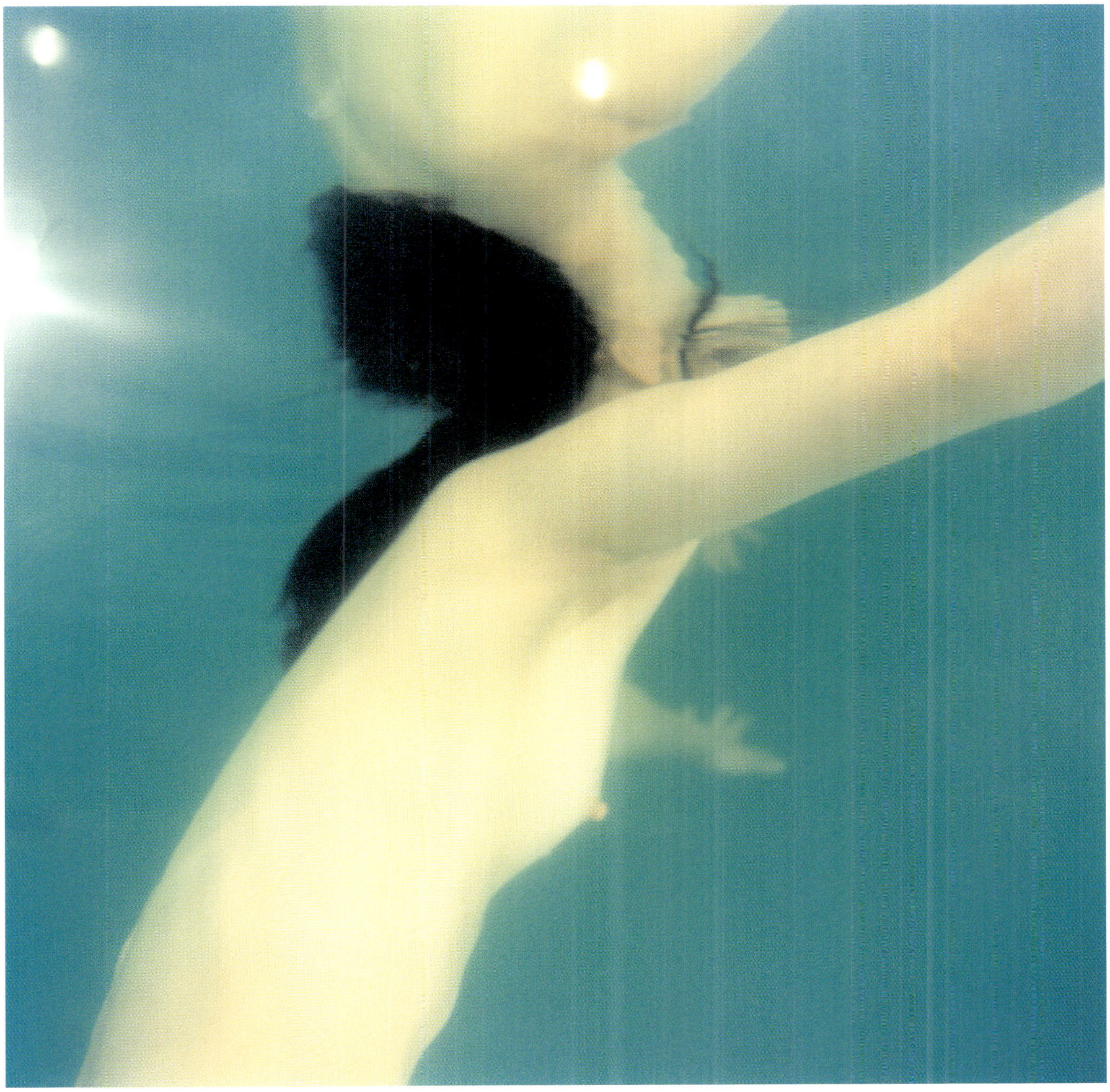

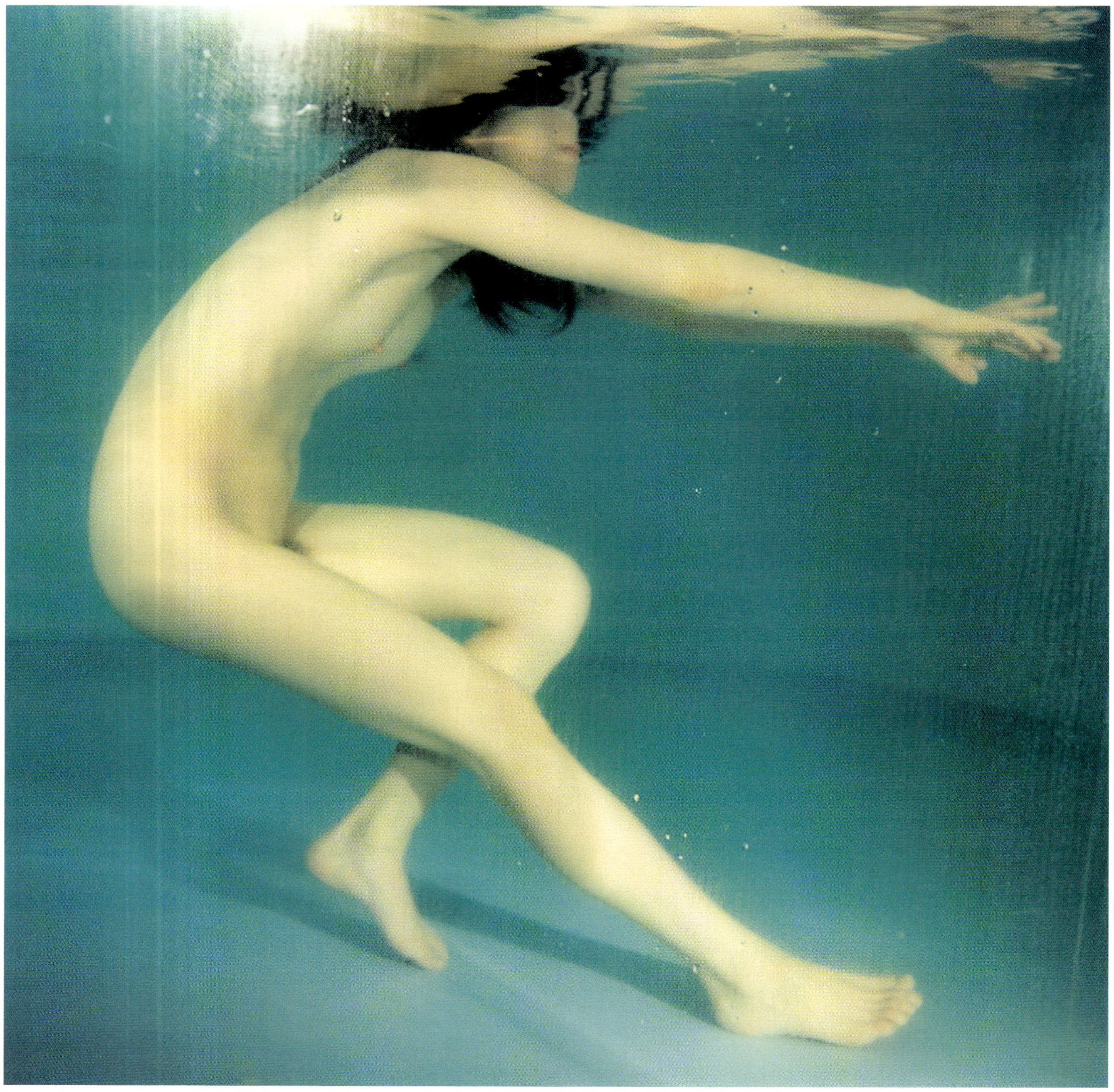

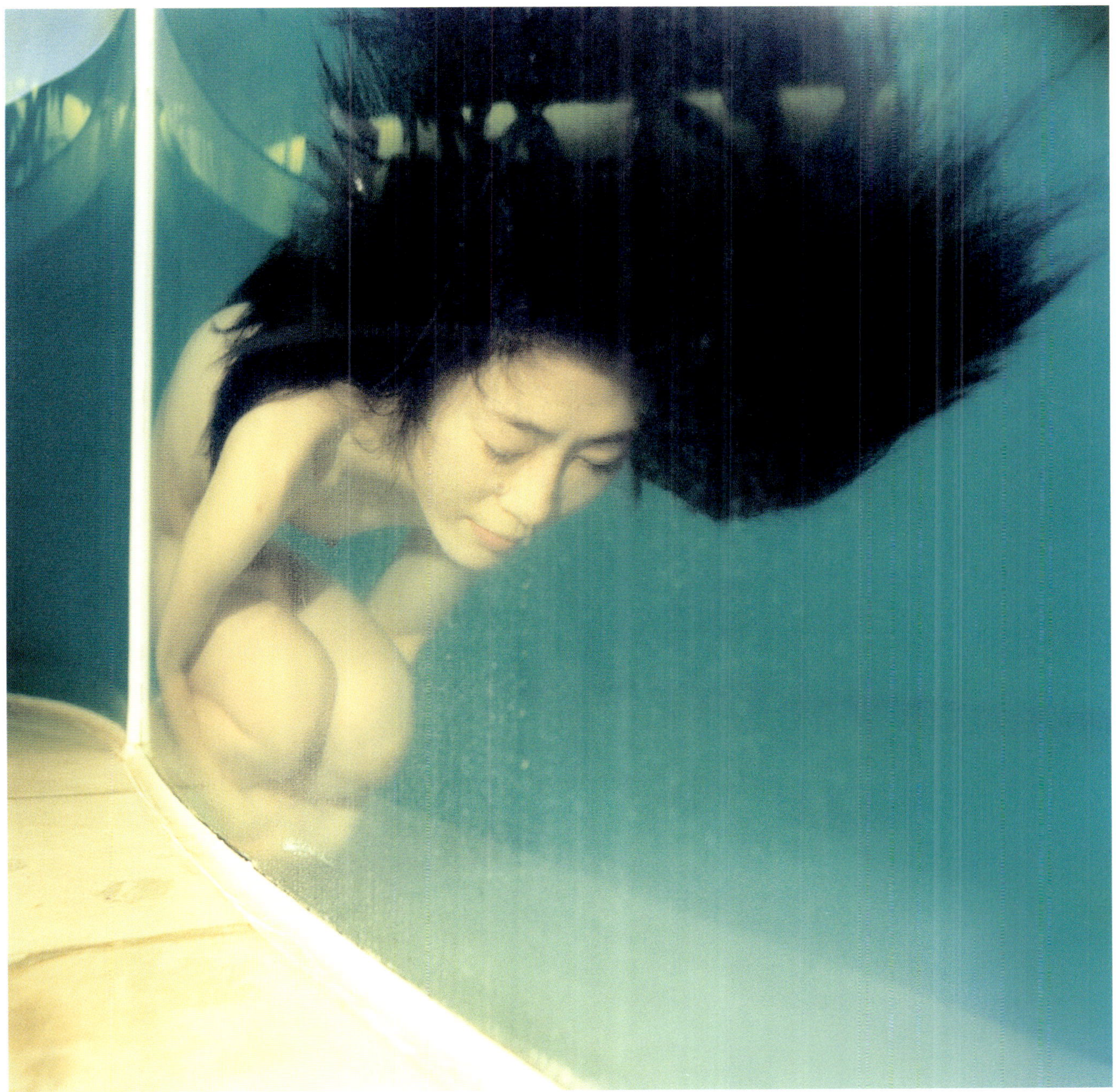

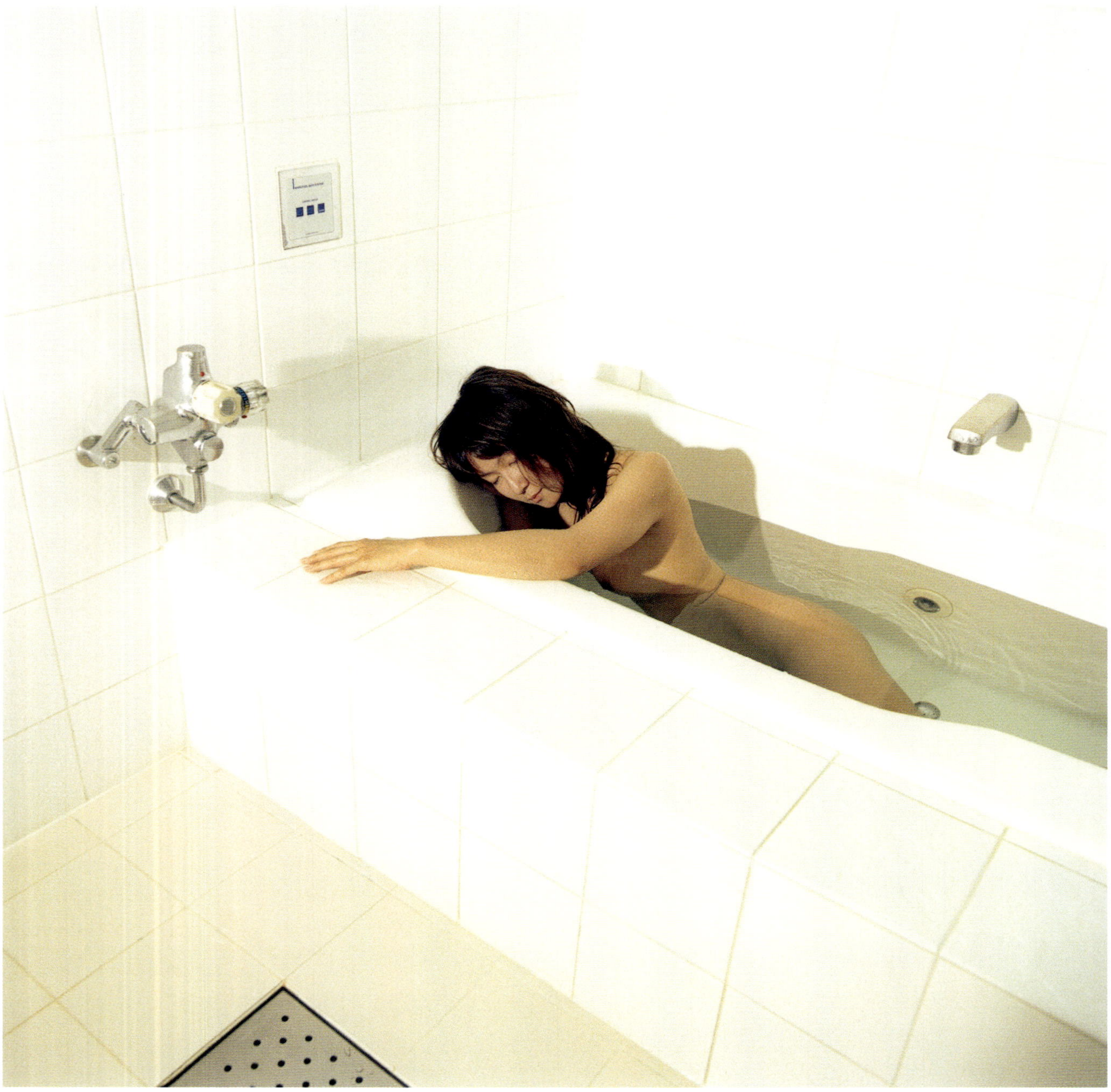

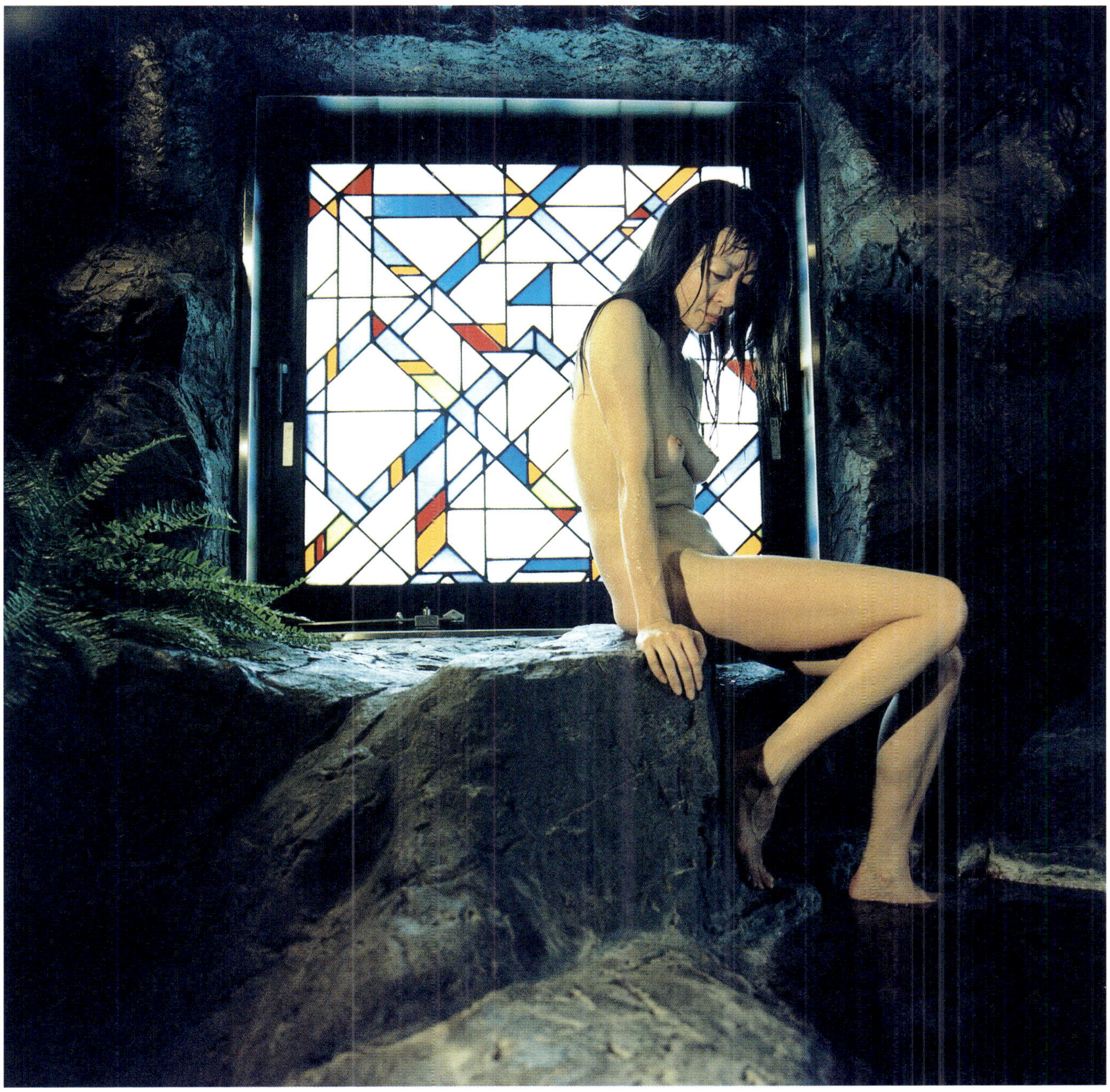

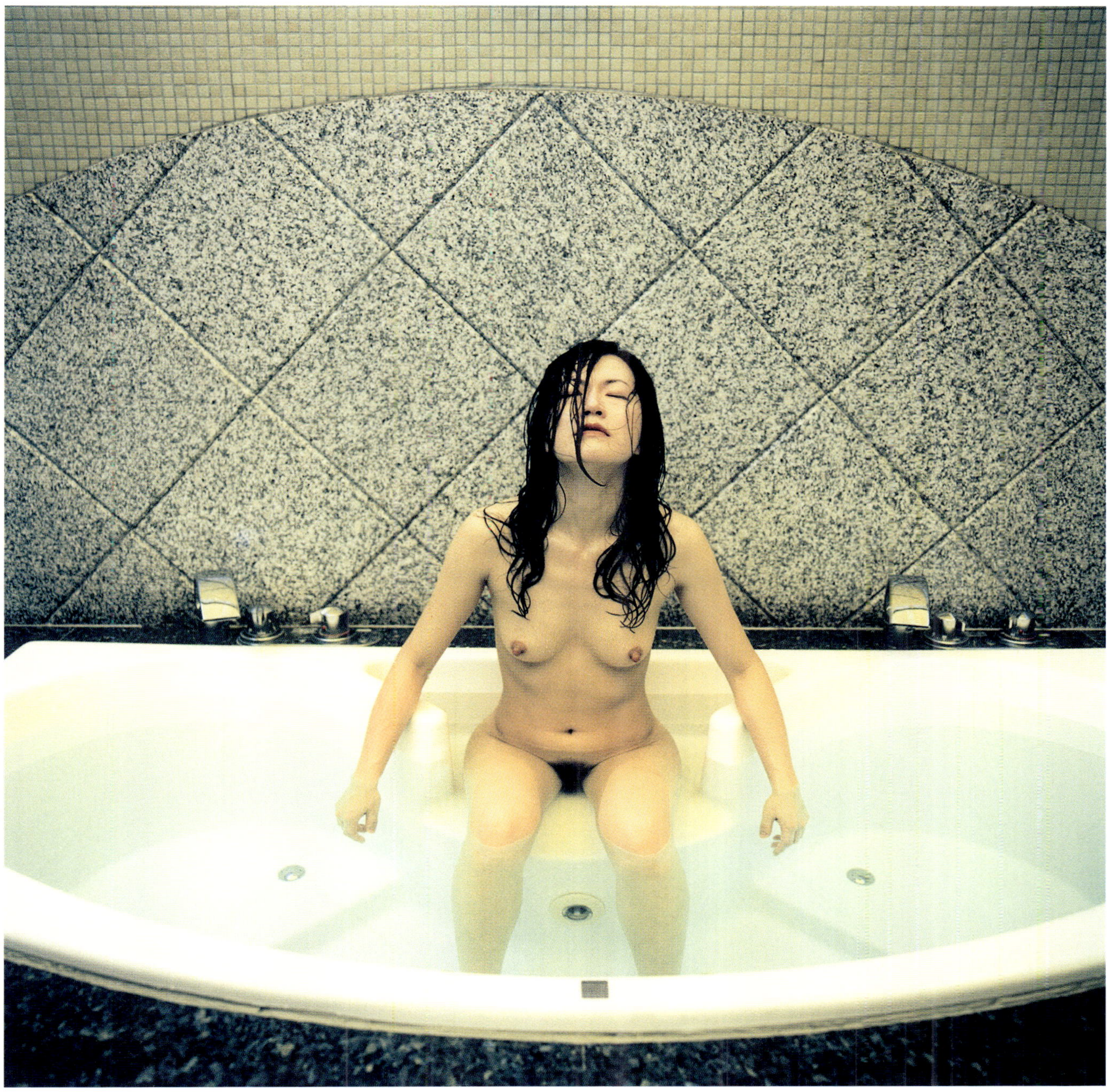

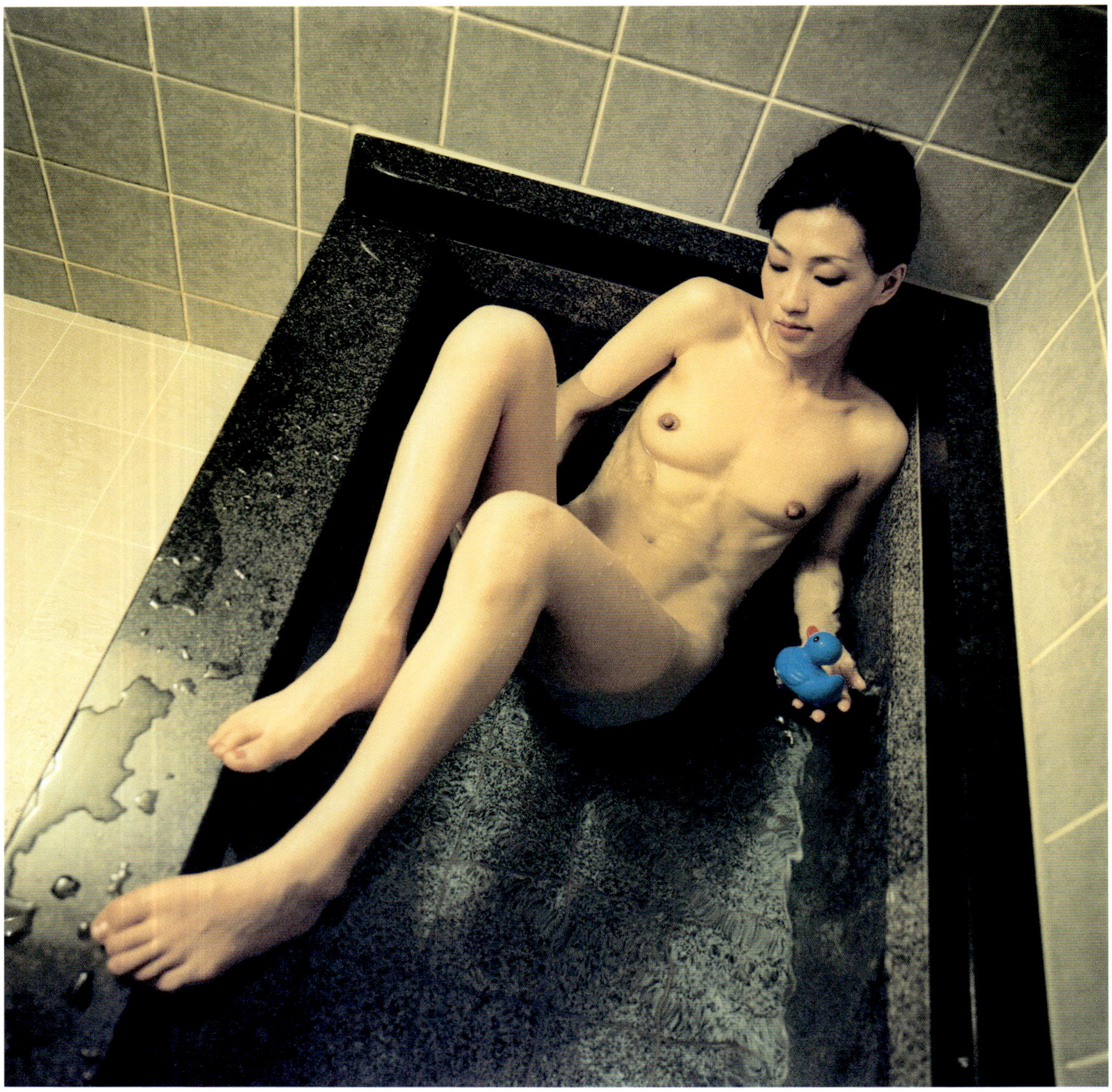

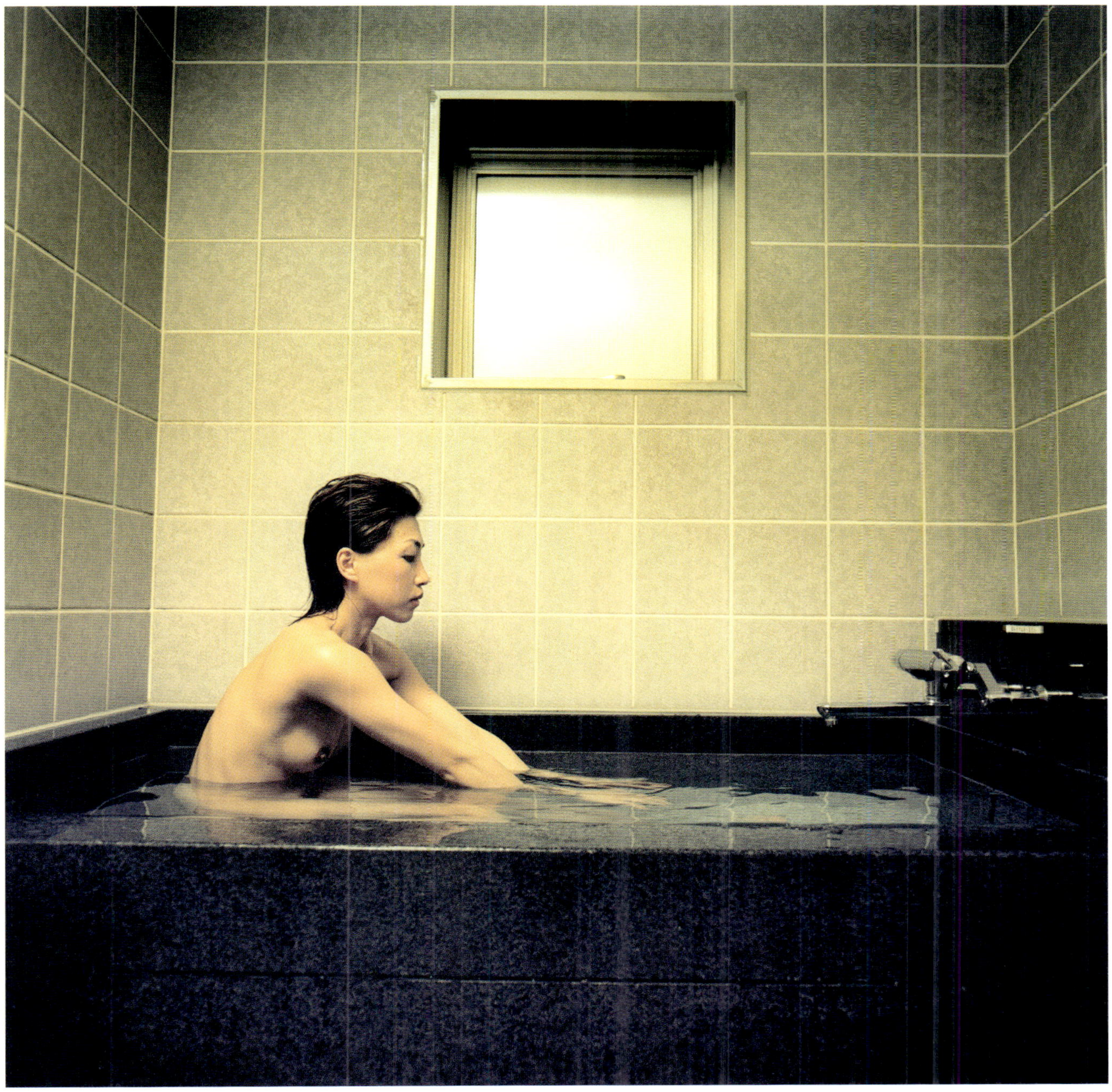

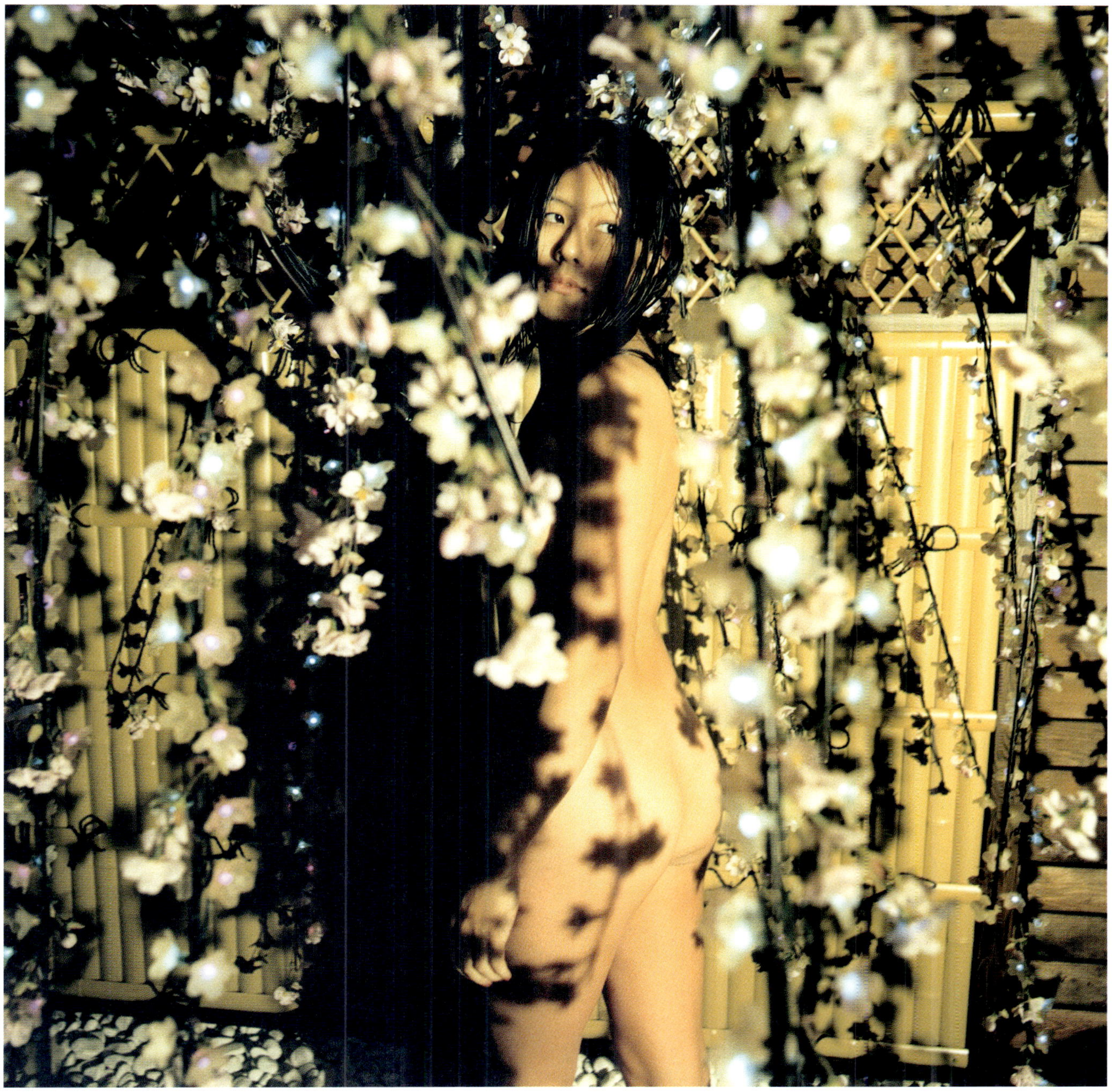

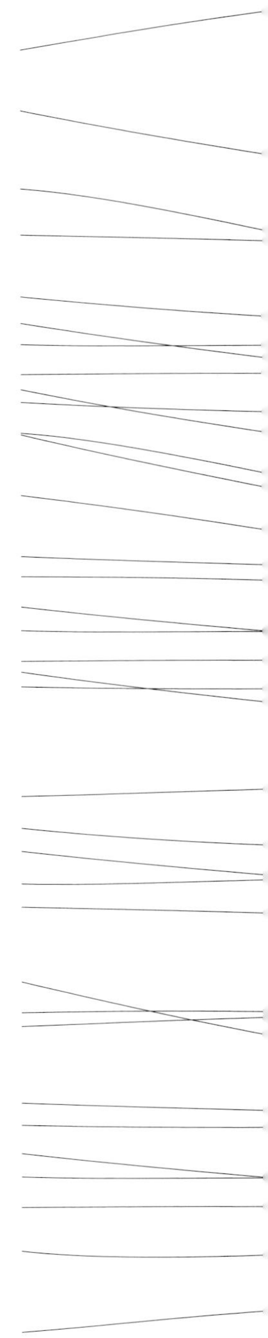

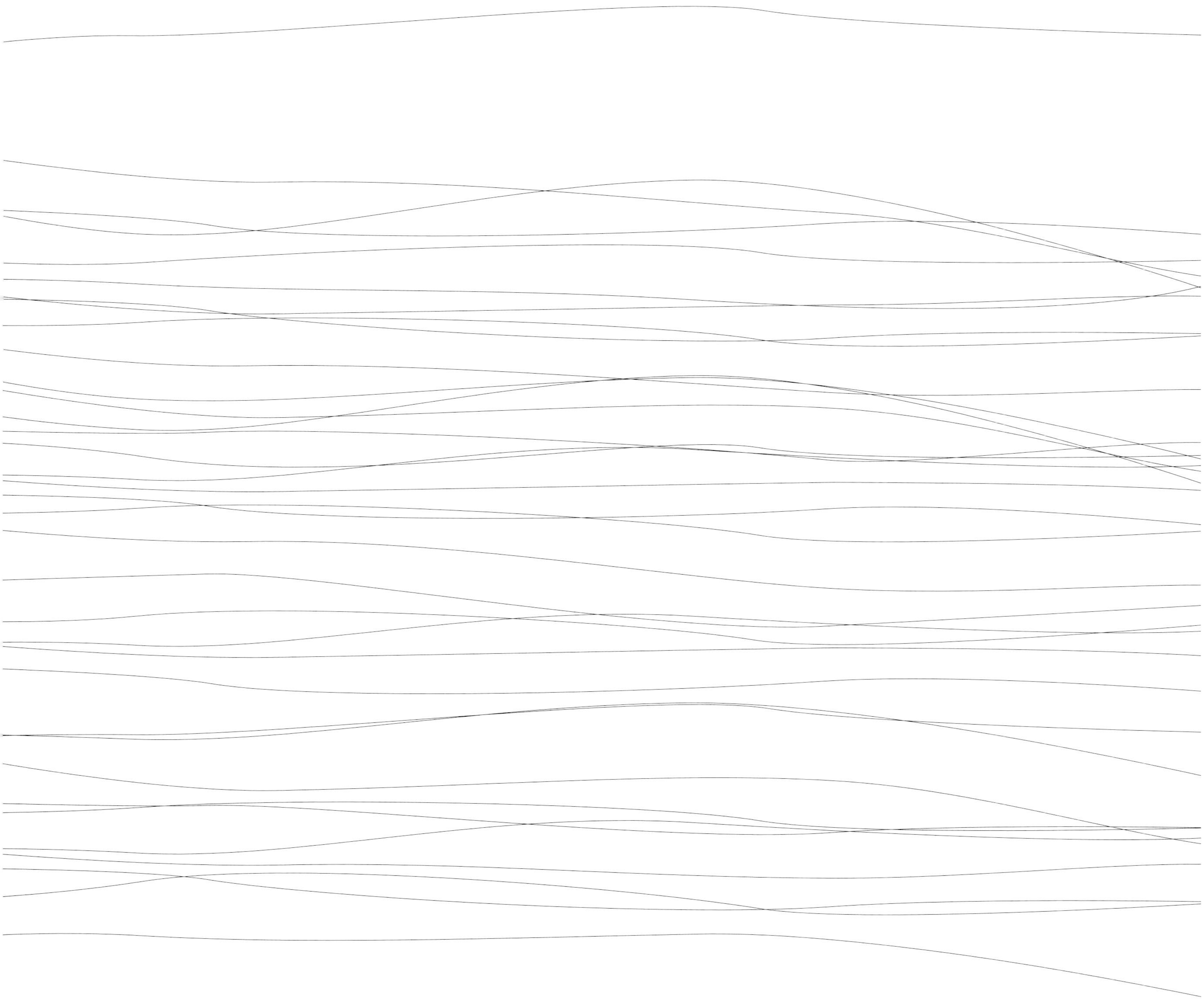

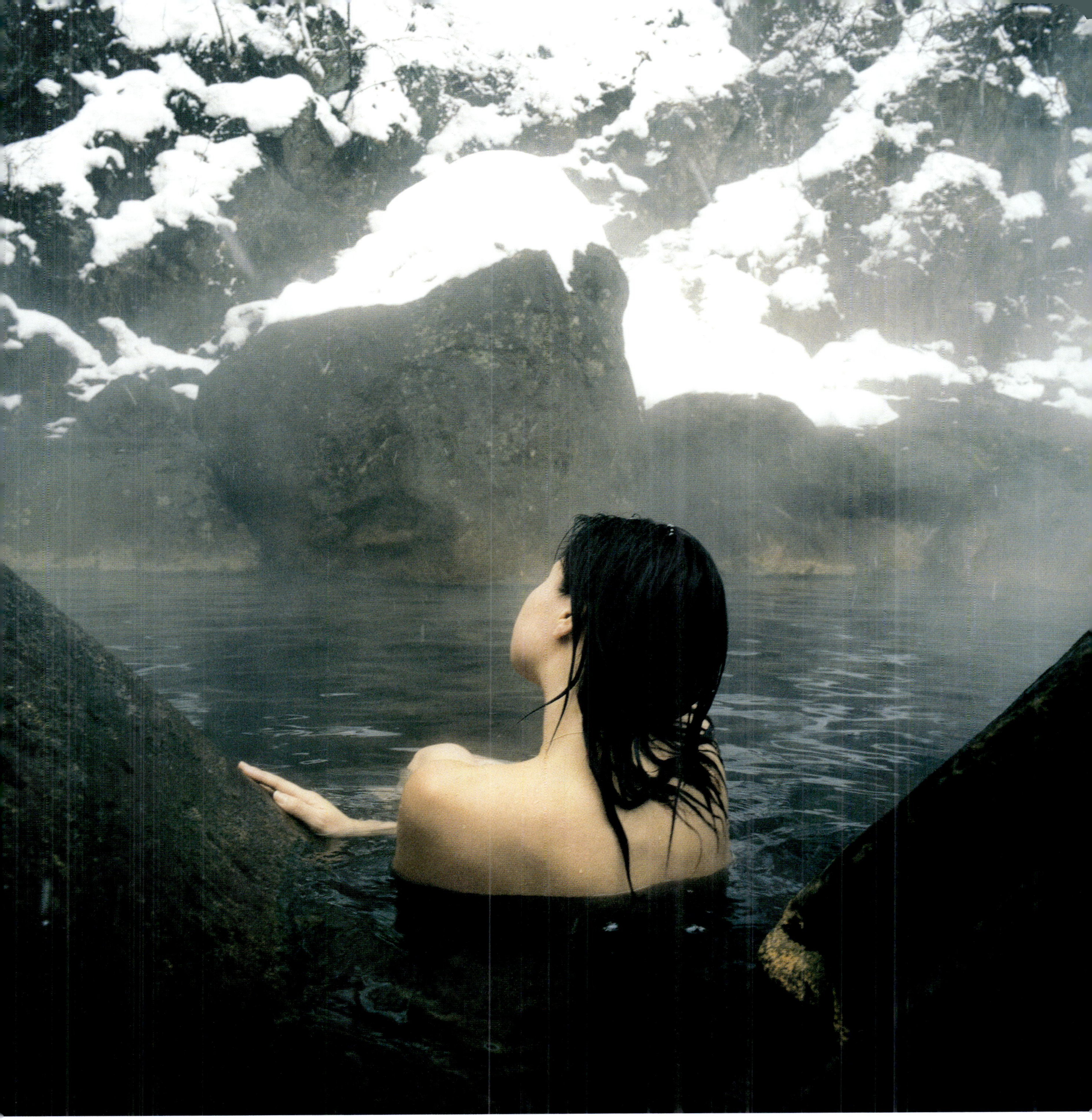

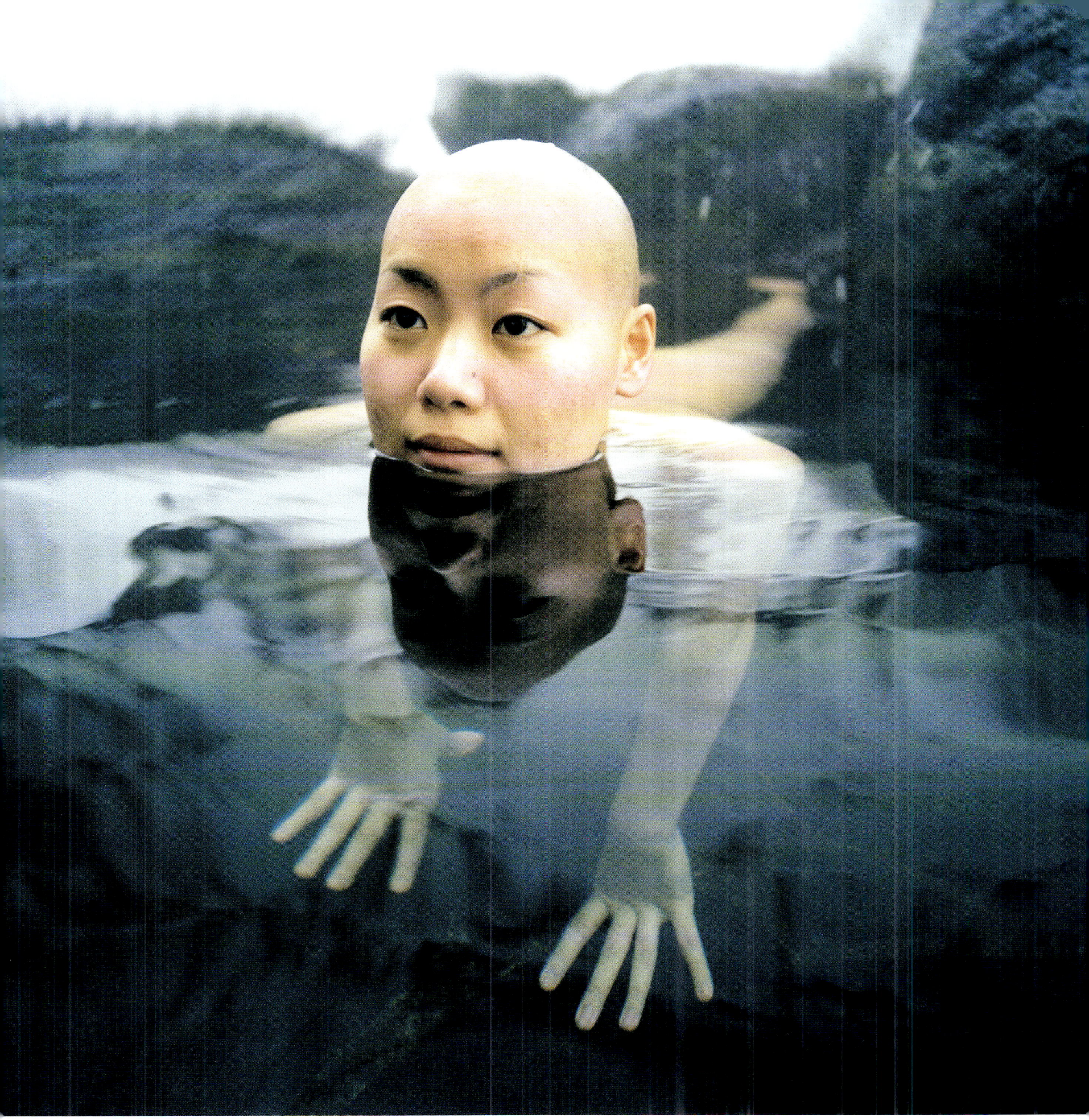

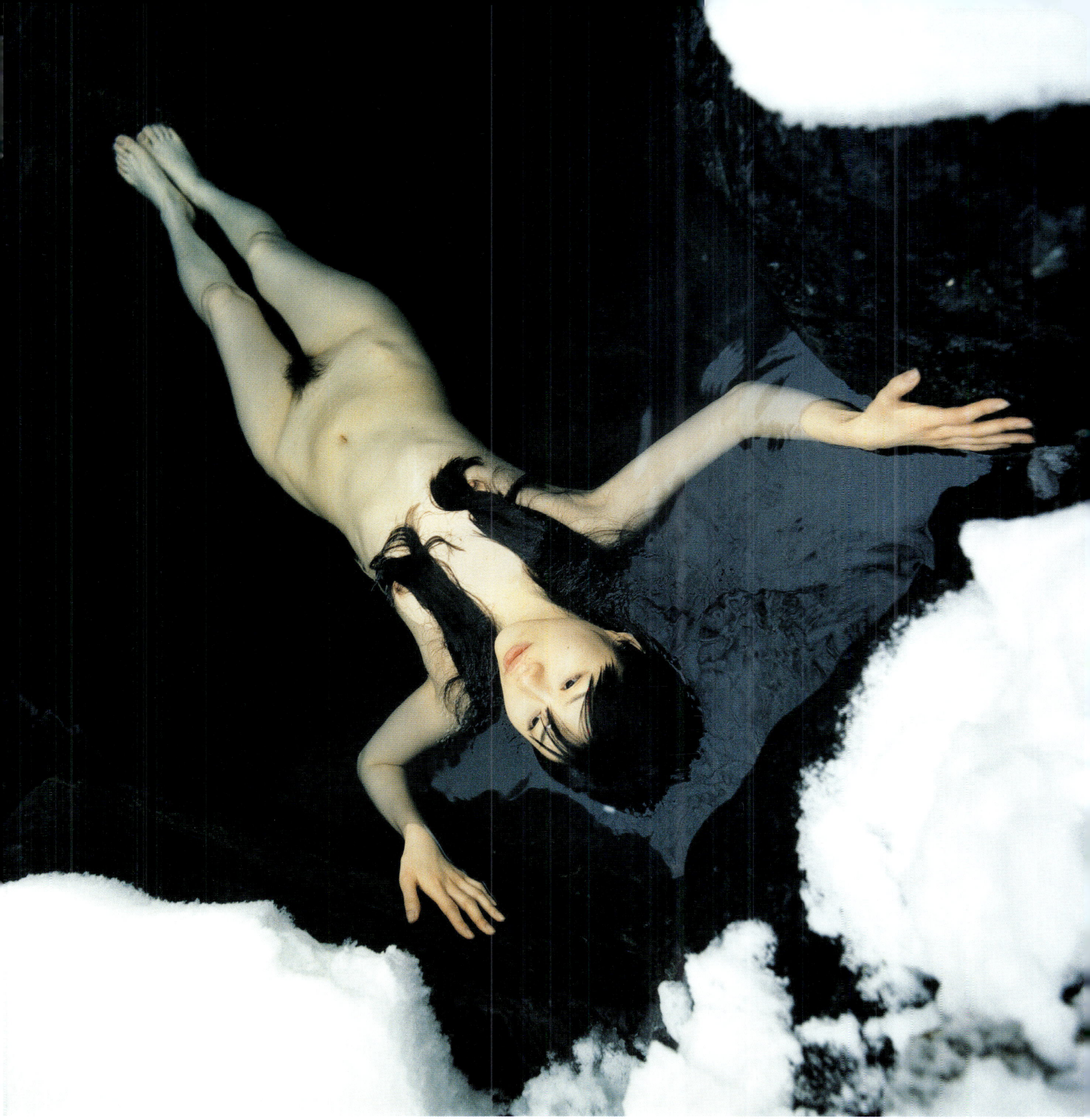

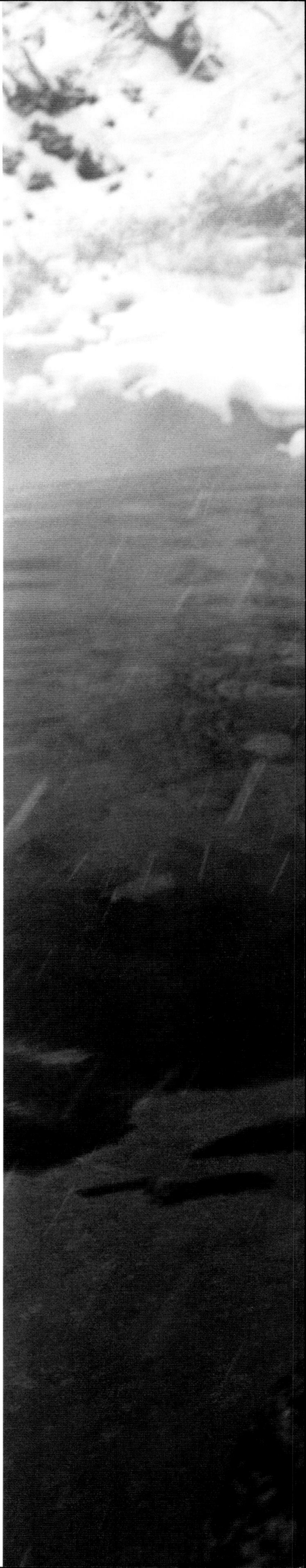

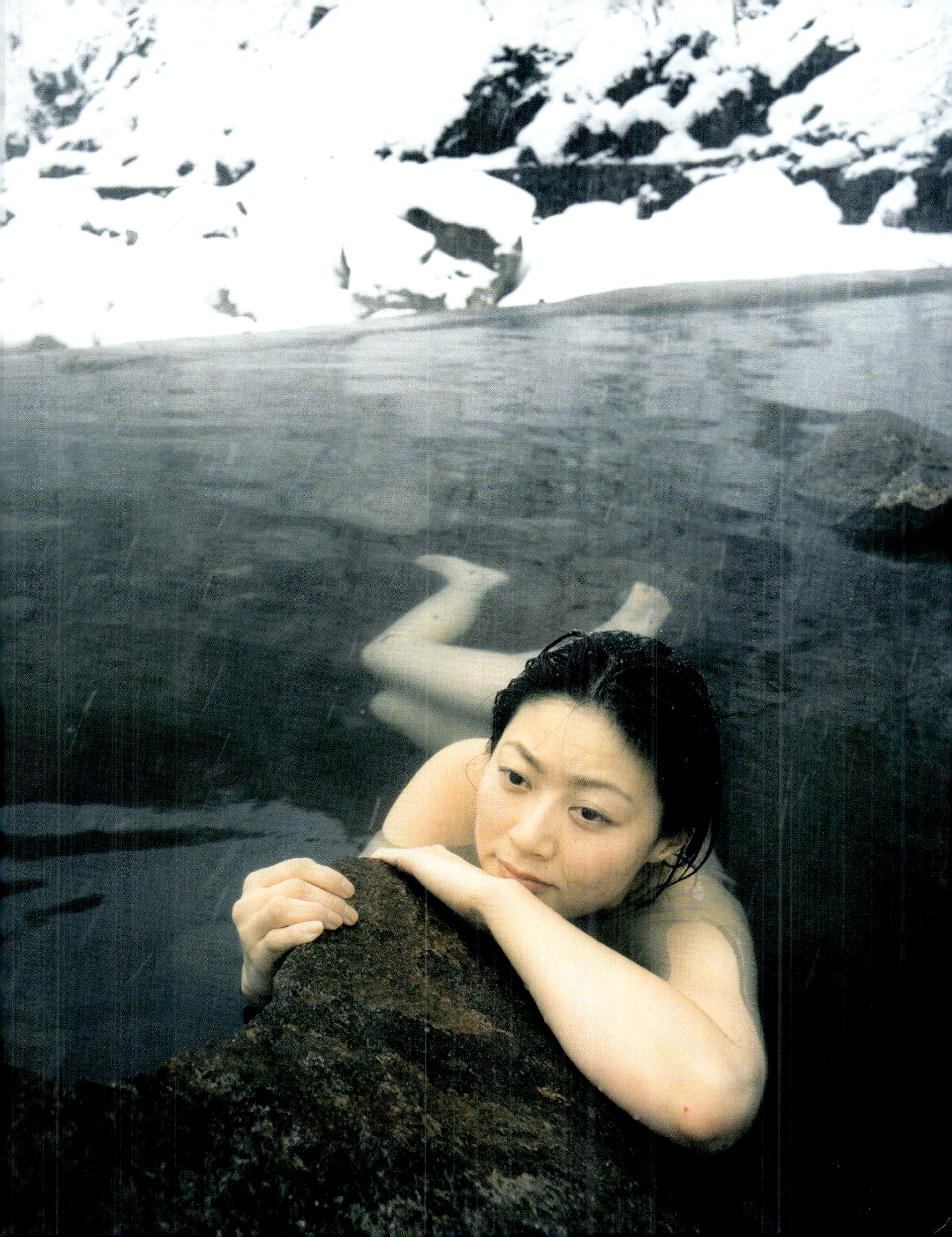

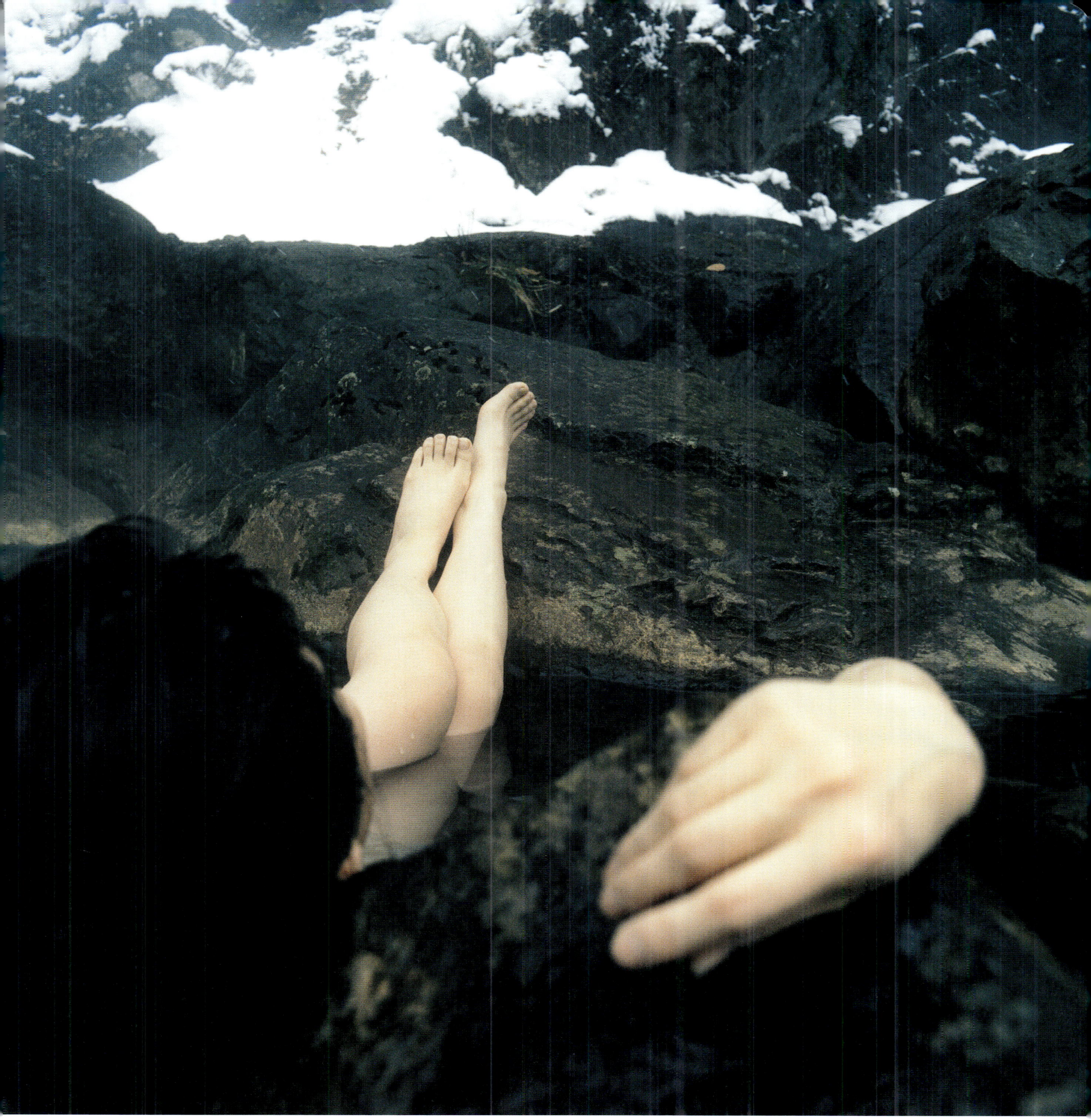

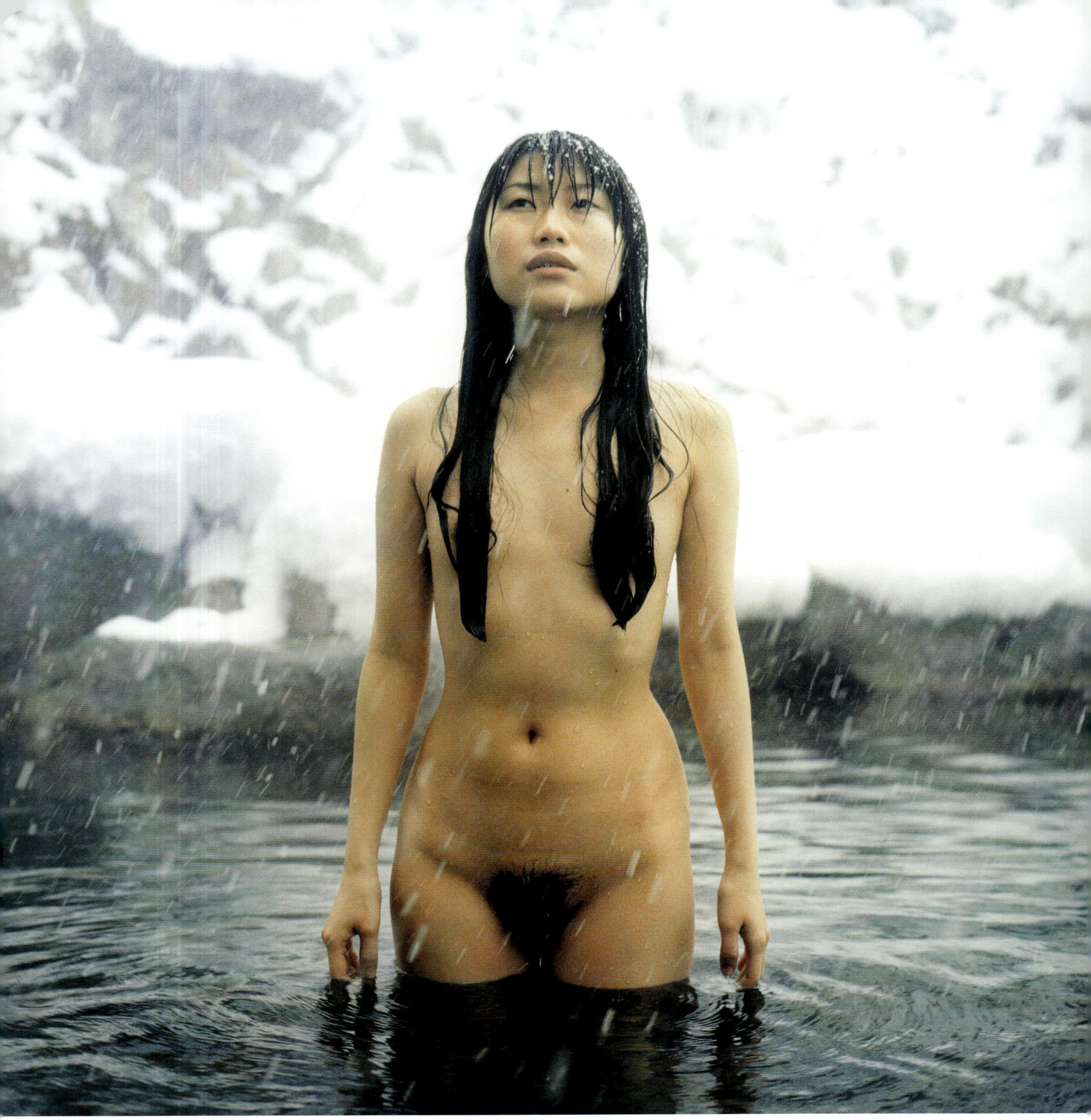

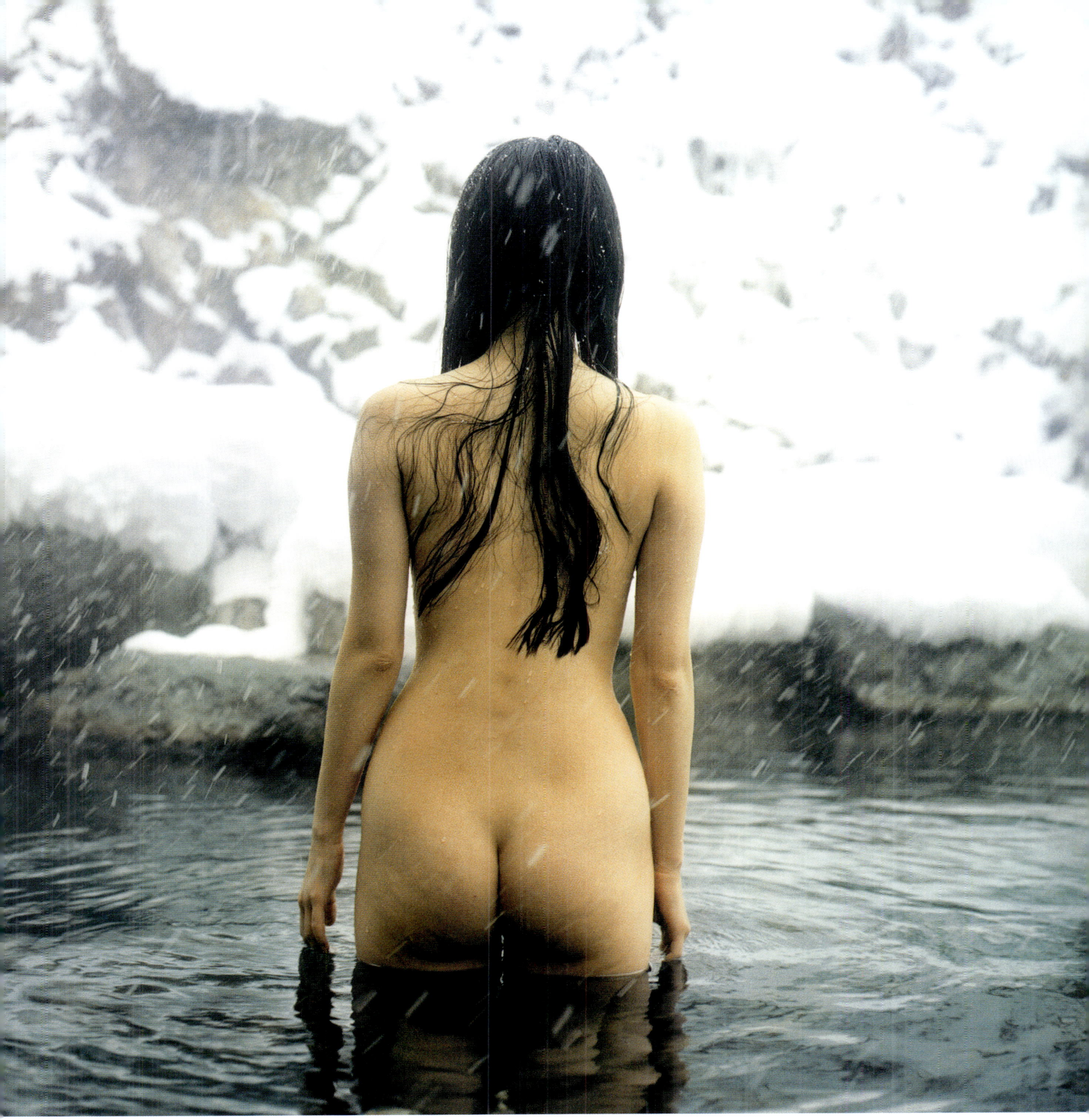

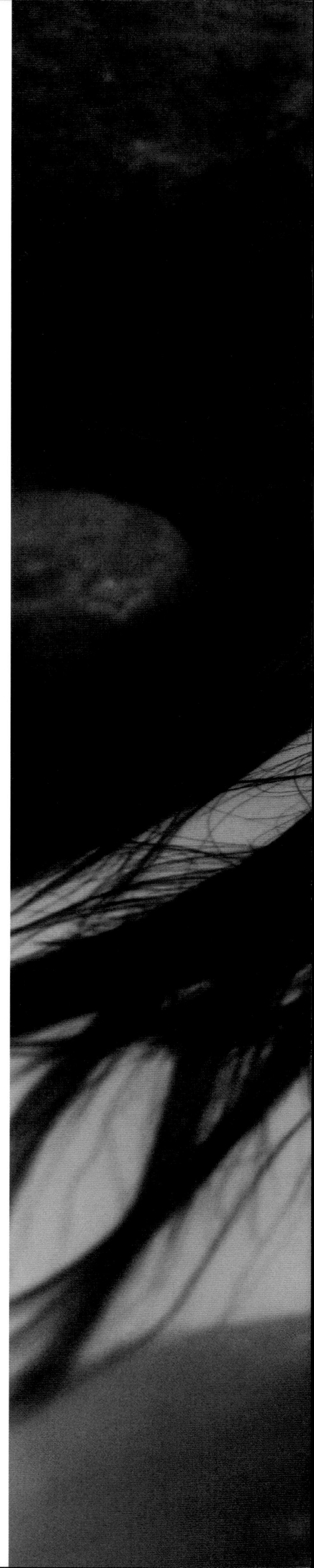

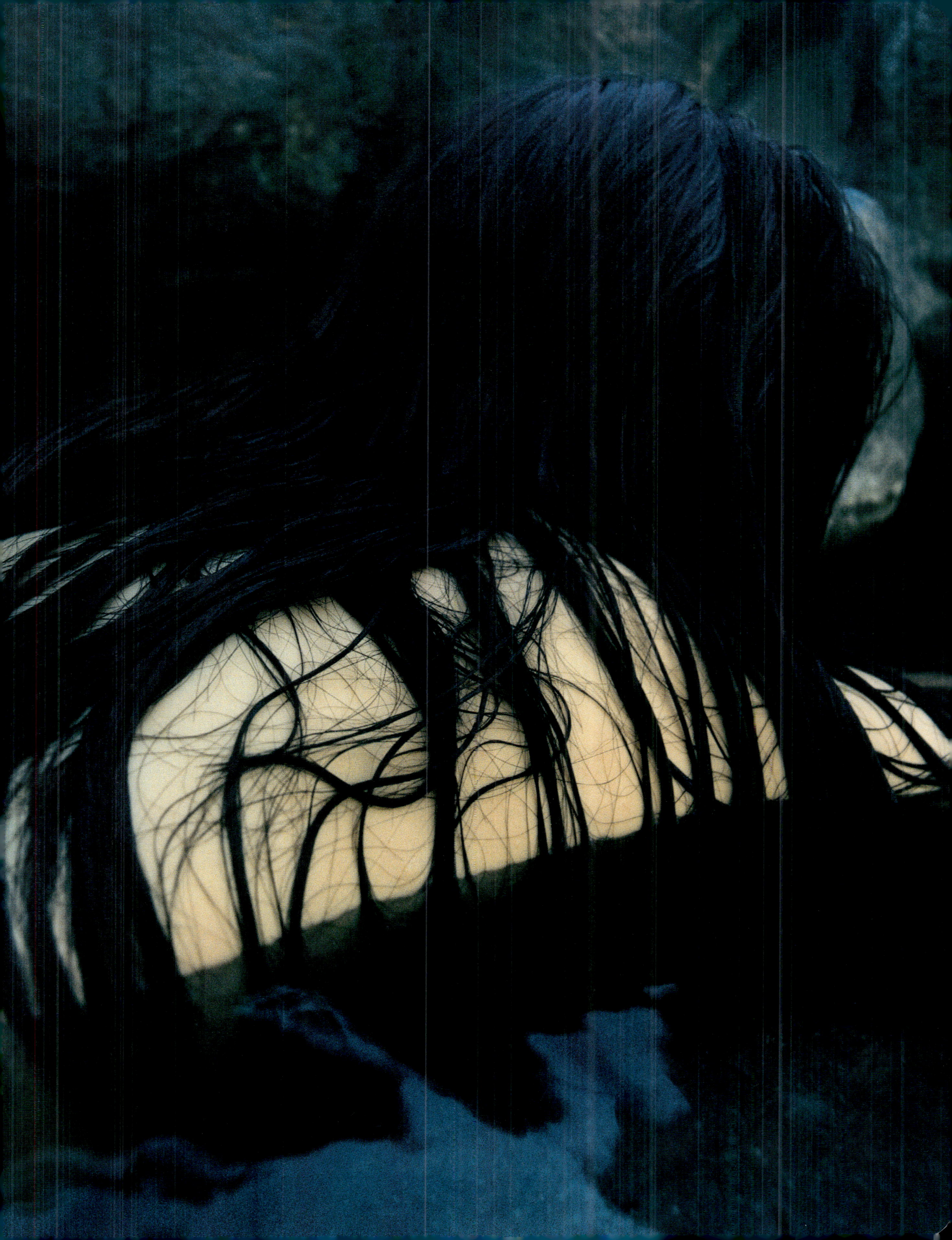

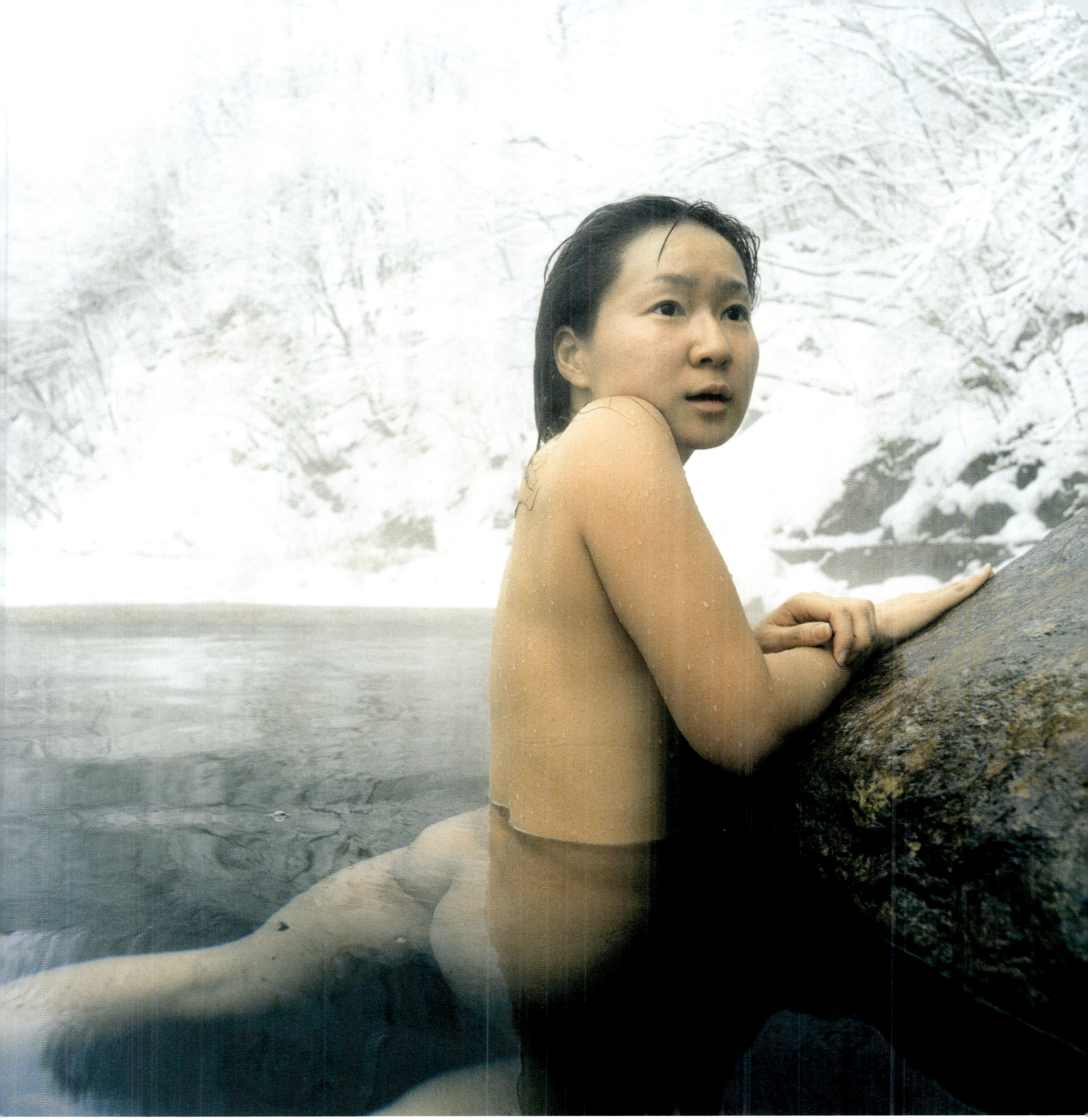

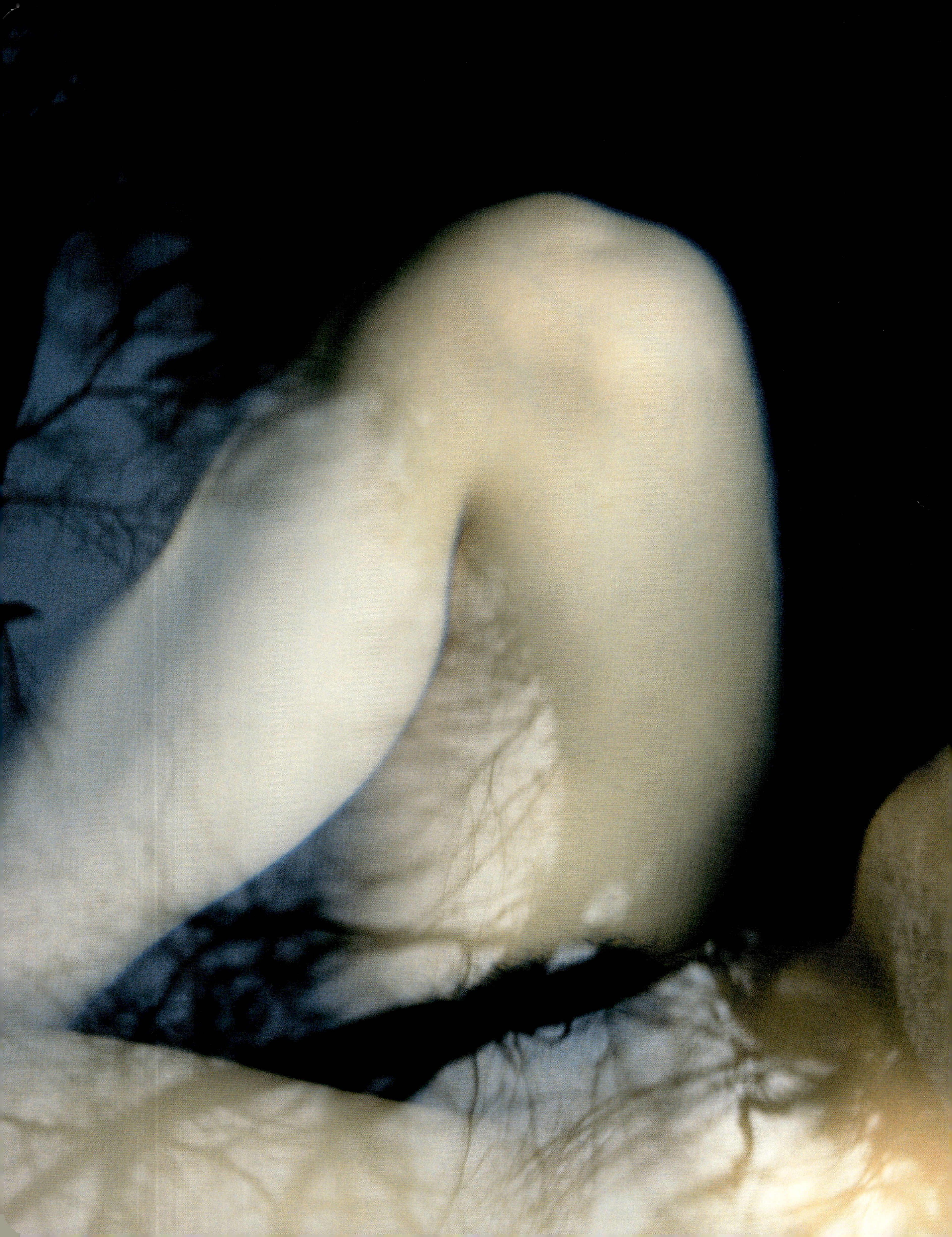

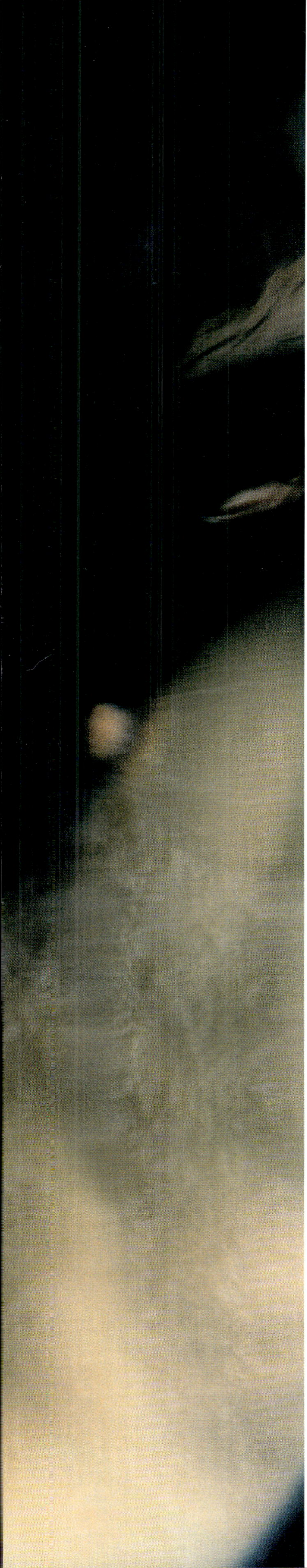

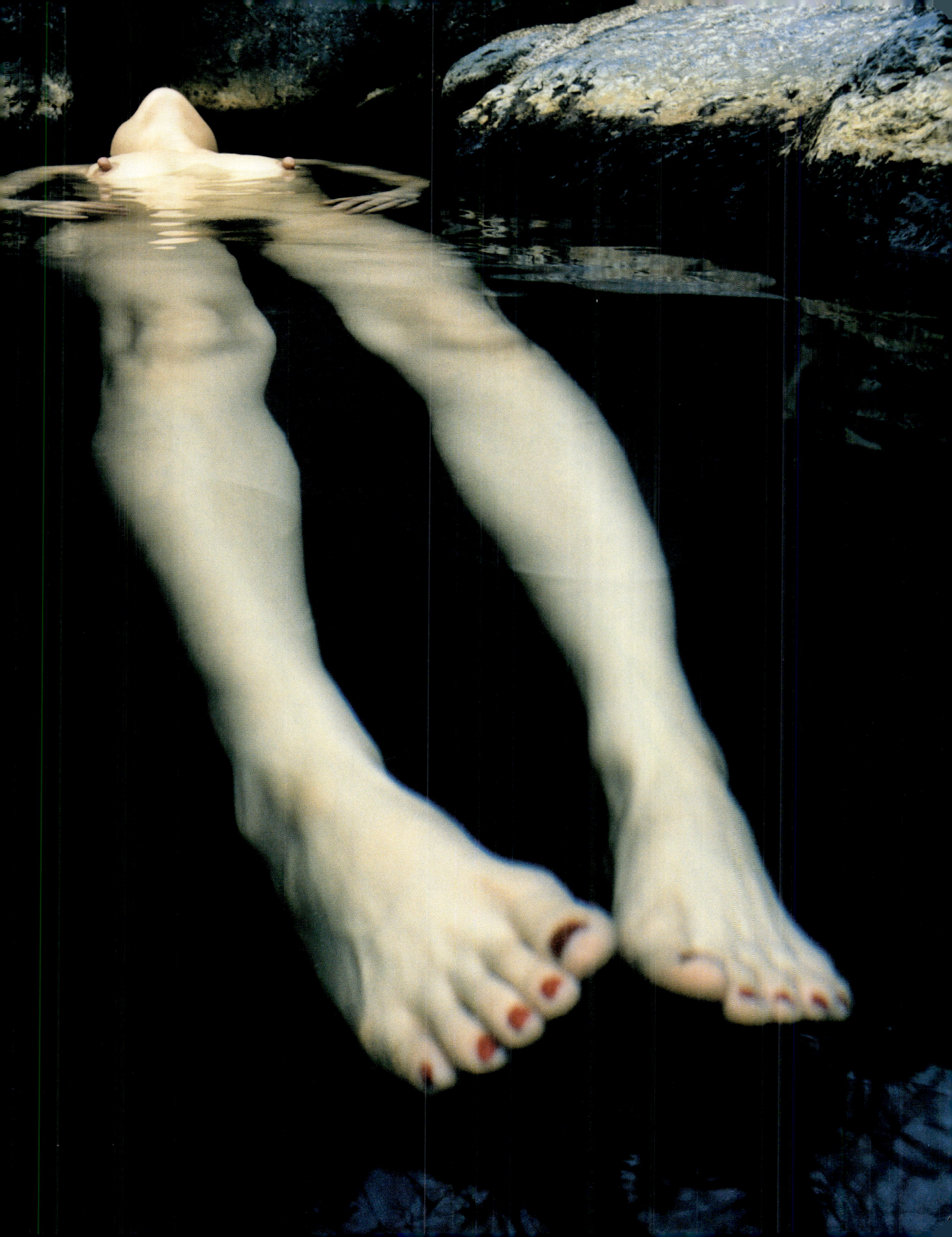

Ces photographies ont été exposées par Phillips de Pury & Company à New York, du 9 au 26 janvier 2007.

These photographs were exhibited by Phillips de Pury & Company in New York from January 9 tc 26, 2007.

これらの写真は2007年1月9日から29日まで Phillips de Pury & Company によってニューヨークで展示されたものです。

Phillips de Pury & Company
450 West 15th Street
New York, NY 10011

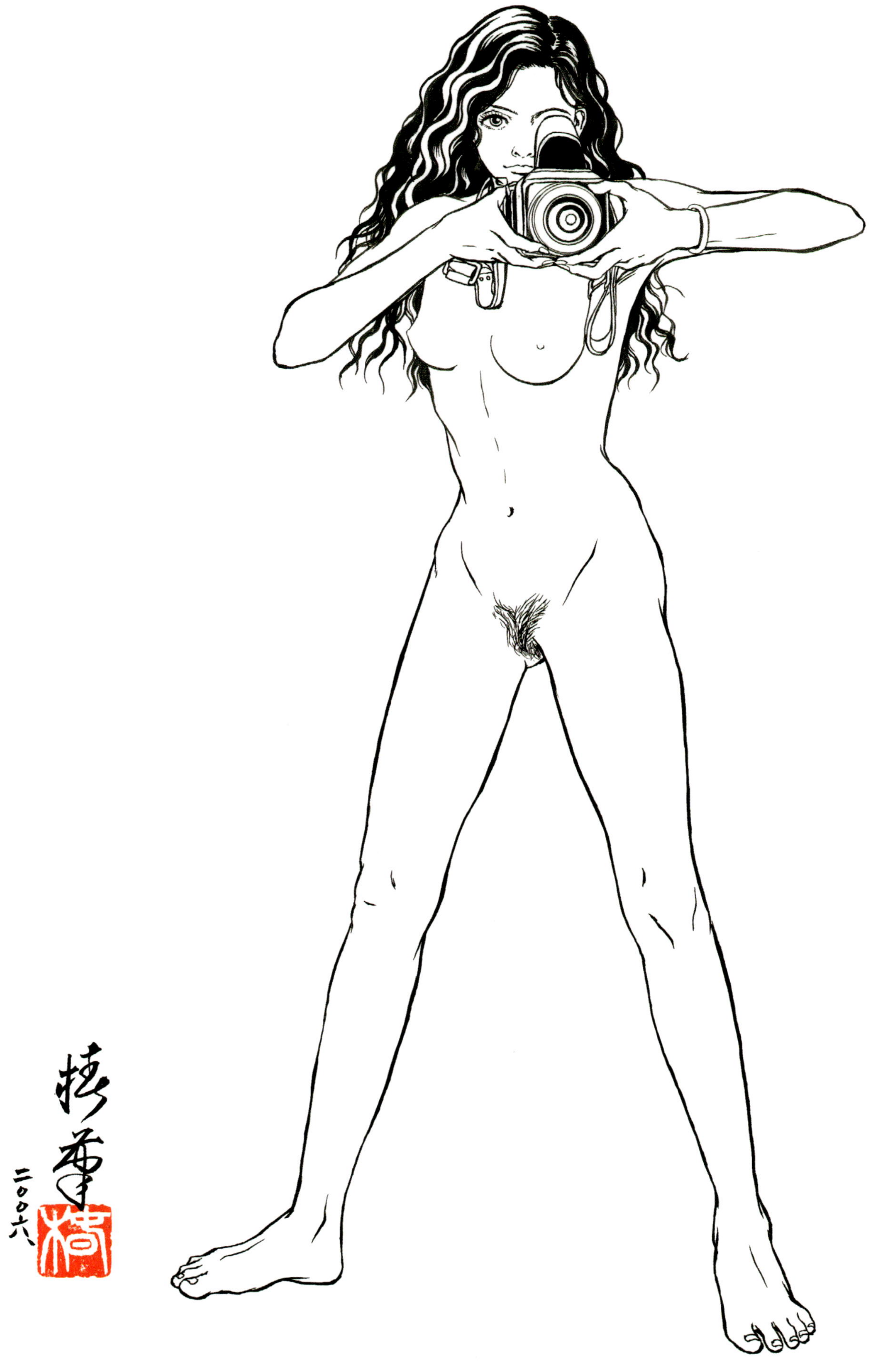
二〇〇六、八

REMERCIEMENTS / ACKNOWLEDGMENTS / お礼

Merci à toutes celles et ceux qui m'ont aidé dans la réalisation de ce livre, en particulier :
/ Thanks to all who helped me in producing this book, and particularly:
/ この写真集の出版にあたってご協力くださった皆さんに感謝します。特に、

Mes parents / My parents / 私の両親 Geneviève & Jean-Claude Reyboz
Mon frère / My brother / 私の兄弟 Julien & Airelle Besson
Ma famille d'ici et d'ailleurs / My family here and everywhere / あちこちにいる親戚
Marion Soulié Liang
Marco Prince

Monique Barbier-Mueller

Simon de Pury

Au Japon, / In Japan: / 日本では
Mario Andrea Vattani
Mari Ikeda
Yasuo Kobayashi
Madoka Mayuzumi
Anna Tsubaki
Hitonari Tsuji

ainsi que / as well as / さらに
Aiko Abe, Philippe et Kozue Bergonzo, Satsuki Chisuga, Jean Cluzel,
Naoki Eri, Laurent Ghnassia, Kanako Hamasaki, Aï Inoue, Wataru Iwasa,
Denis Joly, Hiro Kobayashi, Misaki, Hanako Murakami, Mikako Naito,
Shinji Nohara, Toru Ohta, Masayuki Okamura, Keiko Otani, Chiharu Ozaki,
Brigitte Proucelle, Yuiko Tanaka, Shinobu Terajima, Satoko Yahata,
Junko Yanai, Yumiko Yata, Mayu Yoshikawa

sans oublier / without forgetting / 忘れてはならないのが
Habib Achour, Pierre Amrouche, Thierry Barbier-Mueller, Miquel Barcelo,
Manou et Ralph Bigot, Pascal Bod, Delphine Brunet, Choï, Mamineta Coulibaly,
Carole Daprey, Assane Fall Diop, Ian Flett, Marie-Laure Garello, Luce Garrigues,
Brigitte Govignon, Christelle Grandin, Gilles Guerlet, Gordon Jee, Yuki Kawamura
Salif Keita, Yasuko Koike, Hervé de La Martinière, Jean-François Leroy,
Philippe Levy, Fabien Lherisson, Che Liang, Françoise de Maulde,
Michèle et Michael Mc Murray, Corinne Mazoyer, Mouna Mekouar, Rapho,
Nathalie Roussel, Ryuichi Sakamoto, Sylvie Sanabria, Stéphane Sayah,
Boris & Darius Van Gils, Jérôme Witz, Tiffany Wood.

Préface traduite du japonais
par Sylvain Cardonnel pour la version française
et par Susan Schneider pour la version anglaise.
/ Foreword translated from the Japanese
by Sylvain Cardonnel for the French text
and by Susan Schneider for the English version.
/ 序文の仏訳 : Sylvain Cardonnel
英訳 : Susan Schneider

Haïku / 俳句 : Madoka Mayuzumi
Traduit du japonais par / Translated from the Japanese by / 翻訳
Hervé Collet & Cheng Wing Fun

Manga / 漫画 : Anna Tsubaki

Conception graphique / Graphic design / 装丁 : element-s.net / Jérôme Witz, Gilles Guerlet

www.lucillereyboz.com

Born in 1973, **Lucille Reyboz** grew up in Bamako, Mali, and began taking photographs while a teenager in Senegal. At first she specialized in portraits; during this time she met and photographed a number of artists, including Salif Keita and Ben Harper, and worked for the jazz labels Blue Note and Verve. She published her first photo essays in magazines and newspapers such as *National Geographic, Elle, Le Monde*, and *Air France Magazine*.

The winner of the Fondation Hachette Award in 2001, she exhibited the same year at Visa pour l'image, the international photojournalism festival. In 2002, she and Boris Van Gils made the documentary *Tata* about the Tamberma country in Togo. In 2004, Gallimard published her first book, *Batammaba, bâtisseurs d'univers*. Soon after, she joined the Rapho agency. Today, Reyboz splits her time between Africa and Japan, pursuing her work on the relationships between humanity and nature. In January 2007 her work is on view in New York at Phillips de Pury & Company; the exhibition travels to Zurich and Paris.

Tsuji Hitonari (b. 1959), is a novelist and musician born in Tokyo who later moved to Fukuoka City, Kyushu, and Hakodate in Hokkaido. He dropped out of college to perform with his rock band and write fiction. He received the 13th Subaru Literature Award for his book *Pianishimo* (Pianissimo) in 1989 and the 116th Akutagawa Prize in 1996 for *Kaikyô no hikari* (Lights in the Channel) about impressionable young men detained in the Hakodate juvenile jail. As a musician, Tsuji goes by the Sinified reading of his first name, "Jinsei"; he uses "Hitonari" in his guise as novelist.

ISBN 10: 0-8109-9423-2
ISBN 13: 978-0-8109-9423-2

Library of Congress Control Number: 2006937596

Copyright © 2007 Éditions de La Martinière, an imprint of La Martinière Groupe, Paris, and Abrams, New York

Published in 2007 by Abrams, an imprint of Harry N. Abrams, Inc.
All rights reserved. No portion of this book may be reproduced, stored in a retrieval system, or transmitted in any form or by any means, mechanical, electronic, photocopying, recording, or otherwise, without written permission from the publisher.

Printed and bound in Italy
10 9 8 7 6 5 4 3 2 1

HNA
harry n. abrams, inc.
a subsidiary of La Martinière Groupe

115 West 18th Street
New York, NY 10011
www.hnabooks.com